Using Formative Assessment to Enhance Learning, Achievement, and Academic Self-Regulation

There is convincing evidence that carefully applied classroom assessments can promote student learning and academic self-regulation. These assessments include, but are not limited to, conversations with students, diagnostic test items, and co-created rubrics used to guide feedback for students themselves and their peers. Writing with the practical constraints of teaching in mind, Andrade and Heritage present a concise resource to help pre- and in-service teachers maximize the positive impacts of classroom assessment on teaching. *Using Formative Assessment to Enhance Learning, Achievement, and Academic Self-Regulation* translates work from leading specialists and explains how to use assessment to improve learning by linking learning theory to formative assessment processes. Sections on goal setting, progress monitoring, interpreting feedback, and revision of goal setting make this a timely addition to assessment courses.

Heidi L. Andrade is Associate Professor of Educational Psychology and Methodology in the School of Education at the University at Albany, State University of New York, USA.

Margaret Heritage is Assistant Director for Professional Development at the National Center for Research on Evaluation, Standards and Student Testing (CRESST) at the University of California Los Angeles, USA.

Student Assessment for Educators
Edited by James H. McMillan,
Virginia Commonwealth University, USA

Using Formative Assessment to Enhance Learning,
Achievement, and Academic Self-Regulation
Heidi L. Andrade and Margaret Heritage

Using Formative Assessment to Enhance Learning, Achievement, and Academic Self-Regulation

**Heidi L. Andrade
and
Margaret Heritage**

Routledge
Taylor & Francis Group
NEW YORK AND LONDON

First published 2018
by Routledge
711 Third Avenue, New York, NY 10017

and by Routledge
2 Park Square, Milton Park, Abingdon, Oxon, OX14 4RN

Routledge is an imprint of the Taylor & Francis Group, an informa business

© 2018 Taylor & Francis

The right of Heidi L. Andrade and Margaret Heritage to be identified as authors of this work has been asserted by them in accordance with sections 77 and 78 of the Copyright, Designs and Patents Act 1988.

All rights reserved. No part of this book may be reprinted or reproduced or utilised in any form or by any electronic, mechanical, or other means, now known or hereafter invented, including photocopying and recording, or in any information storage or retrieval system, without permission in writing from the publishers.

Trademark notice: Product or corporate names may be trademarks or registered trademarks, and are used only for identification and explanation without intent to infringe.

Library of Congress Cataloging-in-Publication Data
A catalog record for this book has been requested

ISBN: 978-1-138-65300-9 (hbk)
ISBN: 978-1-138-65303-0 (pbk)
ISBN: 978-1-315-62385-6 (ebk)

Typeset in Sabon and Scala Sans
by Apex CoVantage, LLC

Contents

List of Figures, Tables, and Boxes   viii

Preface   x

1   Introduction to Formative Assessment   1

    Overview   1
    What About Grading?   4
    Three Guiding Questions   5
    Formative Assessment Influences Learning Through
       Feedback   9
    Formative Assessment and Self-Regulated
       Learning   12
    Classroom Culture and Formative Assessment   17

2   Actionable Principles of Formative Assessment   25

    Overview   25
    Middle School Classroom   27
    Elementary Mathematics Lesson   30

Diagnostic Items 33
Self-Regulated Learning, Self-Efficacy, and Motivation 34

3 Clear Learning Goals and Criteria   39

Overview 39
Learning Goals Derived From Standards 40
Learning Goals Derived From Learning Progressions 43
Performance and Product Criteria 47
  Performance Criteria 48
  Product Criteria 51
    Checklists 52
    Rubrics 53
Goals, Criteria, and Self-Regulation 59
Co-Constructing Criteria With Students 59

4 Collecting and Interpreting Evidence of Learning   65

Overview 65
Collecting and Interpreting Evidence as Students Work 67
Collecting and Interpreting Evidence of Learning From Diagnostic Items 70
Collecting and Interpreting Evidence of Learning From Parallel Tests 74
Collecting and Interpreting Evidence of Learning With Technology 76
  Researcher-Developed Tools 77
  Online Assessment Response Tools 79
Evidence Quality 81
Validity in Formative Assessment 84
Reliability in Formative Assessment 85
Fairness in Formative Assessment 86
Using the Evidence 86

*Collecting and Interpreting Evidence of Learning
  From Themselves: Student Self-Assessment 87*
*Collecting and Interpreting Evidence of Learning
  From Peers 91*
Student Interpretations of Feedback 95

5 Taking Action   101

Overview 101
Teachers Taking Action 102
  Continue With the Lesson as Planned 102
  Make Immediate Instructional Adjustments 103
    Modeling 103
    Prompting 104
    Questioning 105
    Telling 109
    Explaining 110
    Directing 110
    Providing Feedback 111
  Make Plans for Subsequent Lessons 113
  *Students Taking Action: Assessment Strategies
    That Prompt Corrections, Rethinking, and
    Revisions Connected to Learning Goals and
    Success Criteria 114*
  Summing Up and Moving Forward 121

Index   124

Figures, Tables, and Boxes

Figures

1.1	Visual Gradation Rubric	6
1.2	Model of Assessment as the Regulation of Learning by Oneself and Others	17
3.1	Scoring Rubric from *Construct Map for Student Understanding of Earth in the Solar System*	45
3.2	Diagnostic Item Based on *Construct Map for Student Understanding of Earth in the Solar System*	46
3.3	Performance and Product Criteria for Seventh-Grade Mathematics Unit on the Pythagorean Theorem	49
3.4	Kindergarten Writing Checklist	52
3.5	Seventh-Grade Persuasive Essay Rubric	57
4.1	Diagnostic Item on Fractions	71
4.2	Scaffolded Self-Assessment of a Persuasive Essay Draft (excerpt)	90

Figures, Tables, and Boxes ix

4.3	*One Big Happy*	92
4.4	The Two Stars and a Wish Protocol for Constructive Peer Feedback	93
4.5	Ladder of Feedback	93
5.1	Patricia Applegate's Sixth-Grade Movement Quality Checklist	120

Tables

1.1	Narrative Gradation Rubric	8
1.2	Examples of Effective and Ineffective Feedback Practices	12
4.1	Ms. Pernisi's Learning Goals and Performance Criteria for Sixth-Grade Lesson on Coordinate Grids	68
5.1	Issues and Questions for High School Geometry Unit	106
5.2	Issues and Questions for Sixth-Grade ELA Unit	108
5.3	Maria Comba's Fourth-Grade Melody Rubric	115
5.4	Meghan Phadke's Third-Grade Recorder Self- and Peer Assessment Checklists	117

Text Boxes

1.1	A Picture of a Lack of Self-Regulation	14
3.1	Guidelines for Learning Goals	43
3.2	English Language Performance Criteria	51
3.3	Guidelines for Criteria	58
4.1	Geometry Online Assessment Response Tool	79

Preface

In this book, we show how classroom assessment can be used to improve learning when we think about assessment as the regulation of learning. Every theory of learning includes a mechanism of regulation of learners' thinking, affect, and behavior: Behaviorist theory includes reinforcement, Piaget's constructivism has equilibration, cognitive models refer to feedback devices, and sociocultural and social constructivist models include social mediation. In one form or another, regulation plays a key role in all major learning theories.

In general, the regulation of learning involves four main processes: (1) goal setting, (2) the monitoring of progress toward the goal, (3) interpretation of feedback derived from monitoring, and (4) adjustment of goal-directed action including, perhaps, redefining the goal itself (Allal,

2010). Research, theory, and practice in classroom assessment emphasize very similar regulatory goals and processes. Defined as a process of collecting, evaluating, and using evidence of student learning in order to monitor and improve learning (McMillan, 2013), effective classroom assessment articulates the learning targets, provides feedback to teachers and students about where they are in relation to those targets, and prompts adjustments to instruction by teachers as well as changes to learning processes and revision of work products by students. Hattie and Timperley (2007) summarize this regulatory process in terms of three questions to be asked by students: (1) Where am I going? (2) How am I going? and (3) Where to next?

Those three questions are also asked by effective teachers in reference to their students' learning. This book describes ways in which teachers and students can address each question, starting by articulating clear learning goals and task criteria, then by collecting and interpreting evidence of progress toward those goals and criteria, and finally by taking action through making adjustments to instruction or learning processes.

We place a particular emphasis on the last stage of formative assessment—taking action to move students toward learning goals. Wiliam (2010) has championed the view that the most useful assessments are those that yield insights that are instructionally tractable. In other words, assessments are only as good as the insights they provide into the next steps in instruction that are likely to be most effective. For this reason, the book includes strategies for using evidence of student learning to adjust instruction toward learning targets—the taking of action.

References

Allal, L. (2010). Assessment and the regulation of learning. In E.B.P. Peterson (Ed.), *International encyclopedia of education* (Vol. 3, pp. 348–352). Oxford: Elsevier.

Hattie, J., & Timperley, H. (2007). The power of feedback. *Review of Educational Research*, 77, 81–112.

McMillan, J. H. (2013). Why we need research on classroom assessment. In J. H. McMillan (Ed.), *SAGE handbook of research on classroom assessment* (pp. 3–16). Thousand Oaks, CA: SAGE.

Wiliam, D. (2010). An integrative summary of the research literature and implications for a new theory of formative assessment. In H. L. Andrade & G. J. Cizek (Eds.), *Handbook of formative assessment* (pp. 18–40). New York, NY: Routledge.

1
Introduction to Formative Assessment

Overview

In Chapter 1, we present the case that carefully applied formative assessment can promote student learning, achievement, and academic self-regulation. We introduce the three guiding questions related to formative assessment—Where are we going? Where are we now? Where to next?—and illustrate them with an example from a middle school classroom. A brief overview of how formative feedback, in particular, influences learning and self-regulation stresses the fact that good assessment is something done by and for students as well as teachers.

This is a concise book, so we will get right to the point: There is convincing evidence that carefully applied classroom assessments can actually promote student learning and academic self-regulation. These assessments include, but are not limited to, everything from conversations with students, to diagnostic test items, to co-creating rubrics with students that they then use to guide feedback for themselves and their peers. Even traditional multiple-choice tests can be used to deepen learning, rather than simply documenting it.

While classroom assessment has always been an important tool for teachers and learners, its significance is increased in the current context of implementing college and career readiness standards (CCRS). Heightened expectations for all students are reflected in the CCRS, which anticipate deeper learning of core disciplinary ideas and practices. Acquiring deep learning is not analogous to a car that moves from 0–60 miles per hour in 3.2 seconds. Deep learning involves students grappling with important ideas, principles, and practices so they can ultimately transfer their learning to novel situations. Teachers need to understand how student learning is developing so that they can respond to their students' current learning status along the way to deeper learning, ensuring that students remain on track and achieve intended goals. Essentially, teachers need substantive insights about student learning during the course of its development so their pedagogy can be consistently matched to their students' immediate learning needs.

Readiness for college and careers not only involves developing deep knowledge within and across disciplines, applying that knowledge to novel situations, and engaging in creative and critical approaches to problem solving; it also involves acquiring learning competencies such as the ability to communicate, collaborate, and manage one's own learning (National Research Council, 2012). Classroom assessment is a key practice for both teachers and students to support deeper learning and the development of learning competencies.

While both major types of assessment—summative and formative—are important for enhancing student learning, research suggests that formative assessment is especially effective. Summative classroom assessment, including grading, is usually done by the teacher for the purposes of certifying and reporting learning. Formative classroom assessment is the practice of using evidence of student learning to make adjustments that advance learning (Wiliam, 2010). Reviews of research suggest that, when implemented well, formative assessment can have powerful, positive effects on learning (Bennett, 2011; Black, Harrison, Lee, Marshall, & Wiliam, 2003; Black & Wiliam, 1998; Kingston & Nash, 2011). When any high-quality classroom assessment is used for formative purposes, it provides feedback to teachers that can inform adjustments to instruction, as well as feedback to students that supports their learning.

As we will demonstrate throughout this book, feedback is the core element of formative assessment (Hattie & Timperley, 2007; Sadler, 1989). Teachers receive feedback about their teaching and their students' learning from evidence they obtain while learning is taking place, and students receive feedback from their teachers, peers, and their own self-assessment during the course of learning. In formative assessment, the purpose of generating feedback from these different sources is to help students take action to move forward in their learning.

This book is about how to leverage the power of formative assessment in the service of good teaching, deep learning, and self-regulated learning. We will summarize what we know about how formative assessment influences learning and self-regulation. We will then introduce actionable principles, and illustrate how those principles have been successfully implemented in K–12 classrooms.

The purpose of the book is to make it possible for educators in every discipline and grade level to amplify the instructional influence of a ubiquitous but typically underpowered process—formative assessment. Doing so is likely to help students become more willing to critique and revise their thought processes and their work. As a result, they will learn more and obtain higher grades and test scores.

You might notice that the last sentence above contains a relatively bold claim—especially the part about higher test scores. We stand by that claim because of what we know from our own teaching, as well as from research on what happens when assessment is used to provide feedback to both students and teachers. When we think about assessment as feedback, instead of just measurement, claims about improvements to teaching and learning make sense. For a content-free demonstration of how assessment as feedback can promote learning and motivation, please see the video on formative assessment produced by the Arts Achieve project in New York City: www.artsachieve.org/formative-assessment#chapter1; scroll to 8:56 on the timeline.

What About Grading?

Unlike formative feedback, summative assessment has gained a reputation for having unintended, often destructive consequences for both learning and motivation. For example, research showing that grades are negatively associated with performance, self-efficacy, and motivation implies that grades can trigger counterproductive learning processes (Butler, 1987; Butler & Nisan, 1986; Lipnevich & Smith, 2008), especially for low-achieving students. Because our grade-obsessed society is unlikely to abandon grades any time soon, the best we can do is attempt to minimize the negative influence of grades and scores on students. Formative feedback can help us do that.

Giving students grades is not formative feedback. For feedback to be formative, it occurs while students are in the process of learning, whereas grades provide a summative judgment, an evaluation of the learning that has been achieved. Unlike feedback, grades do not provide students with the information they need to take the necessary action to close the gap between their current learning status and desired goals (Sadler, 1989). Grades and scores stop the action in a classroom: Feedback keeps it moving forward.

Three Guiding Questions

Sadler (1989) and Hattie and Timperley (2007) characterize formative assessment in terms of three questions to be asked by teachers and students: Where are we going? Where are we now? Where to next? Each question elicits information and feedback that can be used to advance learning. As you will see throughout this book, these questions are the foundation for effective formative assessment; we will return to them again and again.

To illustrate how these questions are operationalized in practice, consider the following example from a visual arts unit that uses formative assessment. Notice how assessment is seamlessly integrated into the lessons in a way that enables actionable feedback for everyone at work in the room—teachers and students alike (Andrade, Hefferen, & Palma, 2014).

Jason Rondinelli and Emily Maddy teach art in a middle school in Brooklyn, New York. They engaged their students in a long-term biomorphic car project focused on, among other things, observational drawing, contour line drawing, and gradation value studies. As students worked

Gradation Rubric

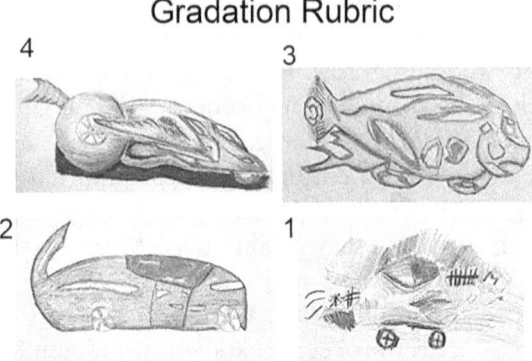

Figure 1.1 Visual Gradation Rubric

on their car drawings, Emily and Jason noted that many of them needed additional instruction about gradation. This observation of student work led them to make adjustments to their instruction. After reviewing the concept of gradation and how it could be used in the project, they involved students in the formative assessment process, beginning with sharing a visual gradation rubric (Figure 1.1; see Andrade, Palma, & Hefferen, 2014, for the color version) created from other, anonymous student artwork.

In order to get students thinking about the nature of gradation—a key learning goal—Jason and Emily asked them to use the visual rubric to write a narrative gradation rubric. A rubric is typically a document that lists criteria and describes varying levels of quality, from excellent to poor, for a specific assignment. Although the format of a rubric can vary, all true rubrics have two features in common: (1) a list of criteria, or what counts in a project or assignment; and (2) gradations of quality, or descriptions of strong, middling, and problematic student work (Andrade, 2000; Brookhart, 2013). A checklist is simply a list of criteria, without descriptions of levels of quality. Jason and Emily presented the visual rubric in Figure 1.1 in order to engage their students in thinking about the nature of gradation while creating a written rubric.

In small groups, students defined a level of the rubric (4, 3, 2, or 1) by comparing their assigned rubric level to the level above or below it, describing the positive and negative uses of gradation in each of the examples, and listing descriptions of gradation at their rubric level. They were asked to describe only gradation, not other aspects of the car such as shape, color, design, or use of detail. By writing the narrative rubric, students were building disciplinary vocabulary, constructing an understanding of an important artistic concept, and answering the question, "Where are we going?"

Once the students defined and described the level assigned to their group, they combined their ideas into the rubric, illustrated in Table 1.1. The teachers then asked them to engage in formative self-assessment of the use of gradation in their drawings of cars by writing their answers to the following questions:

1. Based on the gradation rubric, what is the level of your car?
2. What will you do to improve the gradation of your car?

In this way, students were addressing the questions, "Where am I now?" and "Where to next?"

Their rubric was helpful in answering the "where to next?" question because it was descriptive. If it only used evaluative language such as "excellent gradation/good gradation/poor gradation," it would not have been at all helpful to students as they revised and improved their work. Good rubrics *describe* rather than evaluate (Brookhart, 2013), and thereby serve the purposes of learning as well as (or even instead of) grading.

Table 1.1 Narrative Gradation Rubric

4	3	2	1
+	**+**	**+**	**+**
• It has a cast shadow. • It has gradation on the bottom. • It has a light source. • It goes from light to dark very clearly. • Light colors blend in with dark. • The way the artist colored the car showed where the light source was coming from.	• It has shine marks. • Artist shows good use of dark and light values. • The picture shows gradual shades in the car. • He used light values which helped the car the way he used the shadows.	• There is gradation on the bottom of the door.	• The rims are shaded darkly. • The car looks 3-D.
−	**−**	**−**	**−**
• It has an outline. • Cast shadow is too dark. • Doesn't go from light to dark, doesn't have enough gradation. • Outlined some body parts. • Cast shadow is really straight.	• Needs more gradual value. • Give wheels lighter gradation or darker shade. • The direction of the light is not perfectly directed. • The artists basically outlined the car. • He had more dark value than light values. • The wheels were too light.	• The car is outlined. • There is no shadow. • It's not shaded from light to dark. • There are no details. • The windows have no shine marks. • The wheels do not look 3-D.	• The gradation starts wrong. • The wheels are too little. • Some spots are not well shaded. • The shadow is not shaded correctly.

After carefully thinking about the quality of their work and the ways in which it could be improved, the students revised their drawings using high-quality soft pencils. Finally, they did some reflection by writing their responses to these questions:

1. Did you reach your goals? How do you know?
2. Did you improve the gradation in your drawing of the car? If so, how did you improve it?

These reflection questions represent the kinds of thinking done by highly self-directed learners, who set goals for their learning, regularly monitor their progress toward those goals, and make adjustments to their approaches to learning and to their work as needed.

Emily and Jason were so inspired by the results of the processes of co-creating a rubric and student self-assessment that they expanded their use of formative assessment, including and especially peer assessment, to other units. You can learn more about their work at the Arts Assessment For Learning website, http://artsassessmentforlearning.org/, where you can also find examples from dance, theater, and music. All of them illustrate how teachers have incorporated formative assessment into their practices in order to deepen learning, promote the development of artistic skills, and nurture their students' love of art-making.

Formative Assessment Influences Learning Through Feedback

Constructive feedback played a key role in Jason and Emily's formative assessment practice. In general, research shows that certain types of feedback tend to be associated with learning and achievement (Hattie & Yates, 2014;

Shute, 2008). In order to be most effective, feedback must be related to learning goals and focused on the process of learning. Process-oriented feedback provides students with specific, actionable suggestions they can use (or not use, since feedback is feedback, and not always a mandate). Effective feedback is focused on the task, not the learner ("This story includes a lot of details" versus "You are a good storyteller"). Feedback is formative (not graded), descriptive rather than evaluative ("The claim is clearly stated" versus "That's a good claim"), at the right level of specificity (e.g., detailed and narrative), and aimed at or just above the student's level of functioning. Students report a preference for feedback that includes specific suggestions for revision (Fong et al., 2016).

Hattie and Timperley's (2007) model includes four types of feedback:

1. Task level: Feedback about how well tasks are understood and performed.
2. Process level: Feedback about the main processes needed to understand and perform tasks.
3. Self-regulation level: Feedback about students' self-monitoring, regulating, and directing of actions.
4. Self level: Personal evaluations of the learner.

Hattie and Timperley argue that self-level feedback (e.g., "Good girl") is the least effective because it contains little or no task-related information: It judges the person, not the work or the learning. This claim echoes the work of Carol Dweck (2006), who has shown that teachers can change the way children come to understand their abilities related to an activity simply through the choice of feedback they offer in moment-to-moment feedback: Praising students for their intelligence (e.g., "You are so smart") tends to induce a fixed mindset, while praise focused on effort or process (engagement, perseverance, effective strategy use, or improvement, e.g., "You worked hard to improve this") fosters a growth mindset.

In contrast, feedback about processing and self-regulation are "powerful in terms of deep processing and mastery of tasks," and "task feedback is powerful when the task information subsequently is useful for improving strategy processing or enhancing self-regulation (which it too rarely does)" (Hattie & Timperley, 2007, p. 91). Classroom assessments that provide process and self-regulation level feedback have the potential to be quite effective in promoting both achievement and self-regulated learning (SRL).

Good feedback is also delivered in the right way (supportive), at the right time (sooner for low-level knowledge; later for complex tasks), and to the right person (who is in a receptive mood and has reasonably high self-efficacy—the belief that one can succeed in a particular situation) (Andrade, 2010). Fortunately, feedback can come from a variety of sources, including teachers, students themselves, their peers, and technology.

There is one additional, very important aspect of feedback that is often overlooked: revision. Feedback is most useful when it is followed by an opportunity for the teacher to make adjustments to instruction and/or for students to revise and improve their work. Further, revision by students should be done on the learning or task on which they received feedback—not the next one. This advice resonates with English teachers who spend long hours writing comments on students' essays, only to find they make the same mistakes on the next essay. If, in contrast, students had been able to revise and improve the very essay on which they received feedback, the teacher would have seen improvements in their writing. The extra time spent

Table 1.2 Examples of Effective and Ineffective Feedback Practices

Effective Feedback	Ineffective Feedback
You are asked to compare these ideas. For example, you could try to see how they are similar, how they are different—how do they relate together?	You're a good counter. (Too evaluative and focused on the student rather than the learning)
I see that you have included ideas about the causes for the redevelopment. To strengthen your analysis, think about including more related to the consequences. (Heritage, 2010)	Great work on the painting. (Too general)
I see all the combos that have a chocolate chip cookie nicely organized to support the 6 in your fraction. How can you use one of the strategies we discussed to further support the 12 in your fraction?	You caught the ball; you deserve a star. (Too reward focused) (Hattie, 2015)
One of the axes on your graph is much better than the other. Which one is it, and why is it better?	You are a good student. I am very pleased with you. (Too focused on the student instead of the learning) (Heritage, 2010)

on timely revision can speed up learning in the long run; it is definitely worth it.

In summary, effective feedback provides students with information on which they can take action in order to move their learning forward. See Table 1.2 for examples of effective and ineffective feedback practices.

Formative Assessment and Self-Regulated Learning

Over the last decade or so, people have been looking at the ways in which assessment can help (or hinder) the development of self-regulated learning (Allal, 2010; Andrade & Brookhart, 2016). Self-regulated learning occurs when learners set goals and then monitor and manage their thoughts, feelings, and actions to move them closer to those goals (Zimmerman & Schunk, 2011). Self-regulated learning (SRL) has a long and well-established history of predicting achievement. The reason is pretty straightforward: Self-regulated learners tend to learn more effectively because they have a powerful combination of learning strategies, self-control, and motivation. They tend to set goals for their learning, use appropriate study and thinking strategies, manage their time, seek help when they need it, use available resources, monitor their progress, and switch up their approach to learning when it is not working. In brief, they have learned how to learn.

Take Tracy (see Text Box 1.1) as an example. How well will she do on her math exam? Probably not very well at all. She has not yet learned how to self-regulate her learning by setting goals, monitoring her progress toward them, and seeking help. In fact, she gets in her own way by having self-defeating beliefs about her ability and the value of learning math. Imagine how she would think, feel, and act if she had a self-regulation makeover. Suddenly she would seek out quiet places to study, focus her studying on the material she knows least well, and spread her study time out over the course of a week. She would use the self-tests in back of her textbook, and write down questions about things she still doesn't understand to ask her teacher. If she felt anxious, she would use positive self-talk ("I know I can do this if I keep trying"), take a deep breath, and keep working. Maybe she would use listening to her favorite music as a reward for staying on task during her allotted study hours, rather than as an unacknowledged distraction from studying.

> **Text Box 1.1   A Picture of a Lack of Self-Regulation**
>
> Tracy, a high school student, has a midterm math exam two weeks away. She began to study while listening to popular music "to relax her." Tracy has not set any study goals for herself—she simply tells herself to do as well as she can. She uses no specific learning strategies for condensing and memorizing important material and does not plan out her study time, so she ends up cramming for a few hours before the test. She has only vague self-evaluative standards and cannot gauge her academic preparation accurately. Tracy attributes her learning difficulties to an inherent lack of mathematical ability and is very defensive about her poor study methods. However, she does not ask for help from others because she is afraid of "looking stupid," nor does she seek out supplementary materials from the library because she "already has too much to learn." She finds studying to be anxiety provoking, has little self-confidence in achieving success, and sees little intrinsic value in acquiring mathematical skill (Zimmerman, 2002).

The new, self-regulated Tracy is very likely to do well on her exam. It's the same Tracy—she is no smarter, she has no new mathematical talent—but she knows how to learn, and that is what makes the difference.

Fortunately, there is ample evidence that self-regulated learning can be taught through direct teaching, modeling, coaching, and practice (Schunk & Zimmerman, 1998). Teachers can scaffold SRL by helping students plan, monitor, and evaluate their learning. Planning involves students in setting specific goals for their own learning, as well as selecting useful learning strategies (e.g., explaining new concepts to themselves or others, as opposed to the mindless memorization of facts) and scheduling regular study times (rather than cramming before a test). Monitoring involves students in explicitly attending to whether or not they understand an assignment, reading passage, or lecture, as well as checking their progress toward their goals by, for example, self-testing. Evaluation means assessing whether or not their goals were met, as well as the effectiveness of the learning strategies they used.

You probably recognize the processes described above as typical of your most capable students—yet we rarely teach those processes to the students who need them the most. We believe that formative assessment can scaffold SRL. So far, the link between assessment and SRL is mostly theoretical: In theory practices such as providing feedback about progress toward learning goals would help students take control of their learning. Formative assessment, in particular, is likely to guide students in engaging in key SRL processes, including goal setting (where am I going?), monitoring of progress (where am I now?), and revision of work products and adjustments to learning processes such as study strategies (where to next?) (Andrade, 2013). Emily and Jason used assessment as an opportunity to scaffold goal setting and monitoring when they asked students to reflect on whether or not they had met their goals for the drawings of their cars.

Goal setting by students is influenced by the learning goals and success criteria shared by a teacher or co-constructed by the teacher with students. We will focus on learning goals and criteria in Chapter 3. Furthermore, feedback provided by formative assessment is likely to affect students' monitoring of their progress toward their goals. Revision and adjustment are affected by opportunities that teachers give students to use feedback to revise or elaborate on their thinking, their work, and their approaches to the work.

Nicol and Macfarlane-Dick's (2006) review of the literature on self-regulated learning and feedback led them to conclude that good feedback practice is "anything that might strengthen the students' capacity to self-regulate their own performance" (p. 205). They reasoned that students are less likely to become empowered and develop the self-regulation skills needed to prepare them for learning outside of school and throughout life if formative assessment is exclusively in the hands of teachers.

Figure 1.2 is an adaptation of Nicol and Macfarlane-Dick's (2006) model of assessment. A key feature of the model in Figure 1.2 is that students occupy an active role in all feedback processes, including and especially monitoring and regulating their progress toward their goals and evaluating the usefulness of the strategies used to reach those goals. Processes internal to the learner, including activating motivation and prior knowledge, setting goals, selecting learning strategies, and regulating their thoughts and feelings, are inside the shaded area.

There is some research to support the link between assessment and SRL. Formative student self-assessment has received the most attention. Brown and Harris' (2013) review of research on self-assessment led them to conclude that there is a link between self-assessment and better self-regulation skills because self-assessment promotes students' engagement with the core processes of self-regulation, including goal setting, self-monitoring, and evaluation against standards. Some studies have shown that students who used rubrics to self-assess their learning were more self-regulated than were the students who did not. When students were asked to self-assess their learning *processes* as well as the products of their efforts, they were even more self-regulated (Panadero, Alonso-Tapia, & Huertas, 2012): You get what you assess, as the saying goes.

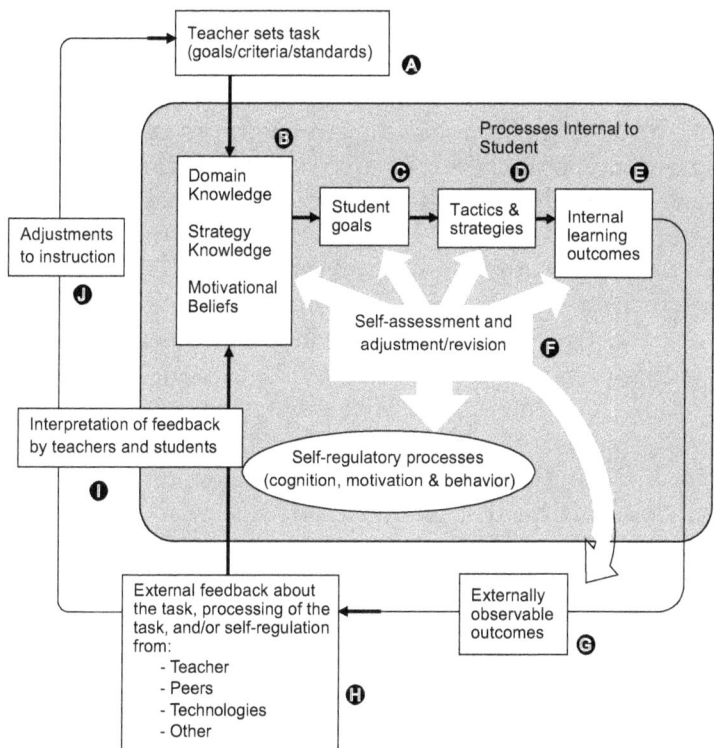

Figure 1.2 Model of Assessment as the Regulation of Learning by Oneself and Others

Adapted from Nicol & Macfarlane-Dick (2006)

Classroom Culture and Formative Assessment

Of course, learning is not just self-regulated by students, but also co-regulated with teachers, parents, and peers (Andrade & Brookhart, 2014; Hadwin, Järvelä, & Miller, 2011): Learning is as much a social as a solo phenomenon. Black and Wiliam (1998) have argued that assessment is also social and that, in fact, "all the assessment processes are, at heart, social processes, taking place in social settings, conducted by, on, and for social actors" (p. 56). For example, trust and respect are essential qualities of a classroom in which students are willing to disclose their knowledge and engage in assessment for learning (Tierney, 2010). In a study of student self-assessment that unearthed trust issues, Raider-Roth (2005) reported that sixth graders carefully selected what they would disclose to teachers, and their decisions about disclosure depended on trust. One girl told of not admitting to being good at writing paragraphs because she did not want the teacher to talk about it in front of the whole room of students, while another stressed the need to get the self-assessment work "right," meaning what the teacher expected. Because disclosure is highly individualized, and trust and respect are essential qualities of a classroom in which students are willing to disclose their knowledge and engage in assessment for learning (Tierney, 2010), teachers have to attend to the assessment environment they help to create, and its effects on student learning and self-regulation.

Research by Bronwen Cowie (2005) has illuminated high school students' perceptions of the assessment environment and has shown that students are very clear about what works for them and what doesn't. For example, students were well aware that their questions disclosed information on their thinking (Wiliam, 1992) and pointed to subtle—and not so subtle—ways that teachers signal, perhaps unconsciously, a lack of respect or sensitivity. One student commented:

> *The worst thing is when you ask a question and [the teacher] belittles you in front of everyone and goes 'Weren't you listening?' or 'Don't you understand that by now?'* (Girl, Year 10)

(p. 147)

Other students noted that this kind of teacher response was amplified if it triggered a similar response from the class:

> Student 1: *If the majority of the class do know what they are doing and you don't then it is really hard because it is like 'Ohhhh (sighs), I [the teacher] have to explain it again'...*
>
> Student 2: *You feel a lot dumber.*
>
> Student 3: *And all the other pupils look at you and you are going* [shrinking down in her seat]. (Girls, Year 10)
>
> (p. 148)

While the teacher probably didn't anticipate this consequence, the students regarded their teacher's and peers' responses as embarrassing and belittling, which negatively impacted their relationships and feelings of self-efficacy.

The students also reflected similar feelings about occasions of teacher feedback, and how it could undermine their views of themselves as capable learners. As one student explained:

> *Because when they say 'You're wrong,' or 'That's not right' or 'Don't do that' or 'Do it this way,' sort of, it makes you think, 'Oh, OK, I stink. I'm just useless at this sort of thing' . . . if you get them to say like 'How do you think you could help this?' . . . you think you can do it.* (Girl, Year 10)
>
> (p. 142)

In fact, all the pupils involved in this lesson observation described the teacher's practice as "rude" or "a put down," indicating that it undermined their inclination to interact with the teacher. Perhaps students' views of an environment that is conducive to productive assessment are best summed up by the student who observed:

> *You need to be able to trust others, to be sure their reactions won't be to make fun, talk about or think I am stupid.* (Boy, Year 9)

(p. 149)

As we can see from the student responses, the social processes of assessment have an impact not only on students' learning but also on their motivation and feelings of self-efficacy (cf. Crooks, 1988). For this reason, it is incumbent upon teachers to create a classroom culture that promotes feelings of trust and respect between teachers and students and among students, and in which each student's contribution is valued. Students watch how teachers relate to them as individuals and to their peers, and they listen to what teachers say and how they say it; "they learn from all that watching and listening" (Sizer & Sizer, 1999, p. xvii). The attitudes teachers express through the language they use and the relationships they develop with their students will influence their students' willingness to participate in assessment (and indeed, learning) and their feelings of self-efficacy.

Teachers can create participant structures and expectations in their classrooms, but the tenor of the students' participation will be influenced by the participant models teachers offer to students. Furthermore, teachers convey their attitudes in how they listen to students as well as how they talk to them. In classroom interaction, obtaining evidence of learning is dependent on interpretive listening—listening closely to what the student is saying to understand the student's ideas, rather than listening for the right or wrong answer (Heritage, 2013).

As Jerome Bruner (1996) once observed, students in school do not simply learn *about*, they also learn to *be*. Bruner's observation implies that students develop identities about themselves as learners influenced by the classroom culture in which they learn. An assessment culture characterized by trust, respect, and feelings of safety among the students to be able to reveal their thinking and ask questions without fear of ridicule or sanctions sets the context for assessment. And when students are invited to be active participants in assessment in the ways described in this book, there is the potential for them to develop their identities as capable, self-sustaining, lifelong learners.

The basic idea here is that, in a classroom characterized by respect and trust, assessment is not done only by teachers. As we begin to think of assessment as something done by and for students as well as teachers, we are likely to increase self-regulation as well as achievement. In the next chapter we introduce three actionable assessment principles that, when implemented well, result in assessment processes that support learning and self-regulation.

References

Allal, L. (2010). Assessment and the regulation of learning. In E.B.P. Peterson (Ed.), *International encyclopedia of education* (Vol. 3, pp. 348–352). Oxford: Elsevier.

Andrade, H. L. G. (2000). Using rubrics to promote thinking and learning. *Educational Leadership*, 57(5), 13–18.

Andrade, H. L. G. (2010). Students as the definitive source of formative assessment. In H. Andrade & G. Cizek (Eds.), *Handbook of formative assessment* (pp. 90–105). New York, NY: Routledge.

Andrade, H. (2013). Classroom assessment in the context of learning theory and research. In J. H. McMillan (Ed.), *SAGE handbook of research on classroom assessment* (pp. 17–34). New York, NY: SAGE.

Andrade, H., & Brookhart, S. (2014). *Toward a theory of assessment as the regulation of learning*. Symposium presentation at the annual meeting of the American Educational Research Association, Philadelphia, PA.

Andrade, H., & Brookhart, S. M. (2016). The role of classroom assessment in supporting self-regulated learning. In D. Laveault & L. Allal

(Eds.), *Assessment for learning: Meeting the challenge of implementation* (pp. 293–309). Heidelberg: Springer.

Andrade, H., Hefferen, J., & Palma, M. (2014). Formative assessment in the visual arts. *Art Education Journal, 67*(1), 34–40.

Bennett, R. E. (2011). Formative assessment: A critical review. *Assessment in Education: Principles, Policy & Practice, 18*(1), 5–25.

Black, P., Harrison, C., Lee, C., Marshall, B., & Wiliam, D. (2003). *Assessment for learning: Putting it into practice*. New York, NY: Open University Press.

Black, P., & Wiliam, D. (1998). Assessment and classroom learning. *Assessment in Education: Principles Policy and Practice, 5*, 7–73.

Brookhart, S. M. (2013). *How to create and use rubrics for formative assessment and grading*. Alexandria, VA: ASCD.

Brown, G. T., & Harris, L. R. (2013). Student self-assessment. In J. H. McMillan (Ed.), *SAGE handbook of research on classroom assessment* (pp. 367–393). Thousand Oaks, CA: SAGE.

Bruner, J. S. (1996). *The culture of education*. Cambridge, MA: Harvard University Press.

Butler, R. (1987). Task-involving and ego-involving properties of evaluation: Effects of different feedback conditions on motivational perceptions, interest, and performance. *Journal of Educational Psychology, 79*, 474–482.

Butler, R., & Nisan, M. (1986). Effects of no feedback, task-related comments, and grades on intrinsic motivation and performance. *Journal of Educational Psychology, 78*(3), 210–216. doi:10.1037/0022-0663.78.3.210

Cowie, B. (2005). Pupil commentary on assessment for learning. *The Curriculum Journal, 16*(2), 137–151.

Crooks, T. (1988). The impact of classroom evaluation practices on pupils. *Review of Educational Research, 58*(14), 438–481.

Dweck, C. (2006). *Mindset: The new psychology of success*. New York: Random House.

Fong, C., Schallert, D., Williams, K., Williamson, Z., Lin, S., Chen, L.-H., & Kim, Y. (2016). *Making feedback constructive: The interplay of undergraduates' mastery goal orientation with feedback specificity and friendliness*. Paper presented at the annual meeting of the American Educational Research Association, Washington, DC.

Hadwin, A., Järvelä, S., & Miller, M. (2011). Self-regulated, co-regulated, and socially shared regulation of learning. In B. Zimmerman &

D. Schunk (Eds.), *Handbook of self-regulation of learning and performance* (pp. 65–86). New York: Routledge.

Hattie, J., & Timperley, H. (2007). The power of feedback. *Review of Educational Research, 77*, 81–112.

Hattie, J., & Yates, G. (2014). *Visible learning and the science of how we learn*. New York, NY: Routledge.

Heritage, M. (2010). *Formative assessment and next-generation assessment systems: Are we losing an opportunity?* Washington, DC: The Council of Chief State School Officers.

Heritage, M. (2013). *Formative assessment: A process of inquiry and action*. Cambridge, MA: Harvard Education Press.

Kingston, N., & Nash, B. (2011). Formative assessment: A meta-analysis and a call for research. *Educational measurement: Issues and practice, 30*(4), 28–37.

Lipnevich, A. A., & Smith, J. K. (2008). Response to assessment feedback: The effects of grades, praise, and source of information. *ETS Research Report Series, 2008*(1), i-57.

National Research Council. (2012). *Education for life and work: Developing transferable knowledge and skills in the 21st century.* Retrieved July 1, 2011 from www.nationalacademies.org/dbasse

Nicol, D. J., & Macfarlane-Dick, D. (2006). Formative assessment and self-regulated learning: A model and seven principles of good feedback practice. *Studies in Higher Education, 31*(2), 199–218.

Panadero, E., Alonso-Tapia, J., & Huertas, J. A. (2012). Rubrics and self-assessment scripts effects on self-regulation, learning and self-efficacy in secondary education. *Learning and Individual Differences, 22*(6), 806–813. doi:10.1016/j.lin-dif.2012.04.007.

Raider-Roth, M. B. (2005). Trusting what you know: Negotiating the relational context of classroom life. *Teachers College Record, 107*(4), 587–628.

Sadler, D. R. (1989). Formative assessment and the design of instructional strategies. *Instructional Science, 18*, 119–144.

Schunk, D., & Zimmerman, B. (Eds.). (1998). *Self-regulated learning: From teaching to self-reflective practice*. New York, NY: Guilford Press.

Shute, V. (2008). Focus on formative feedback. *Review of Educational Research, 78*(1), 153–189.

Sizer, T. R., & Sizer, N. F. (1999). *The students are watching: Schools and the moral contract*. Boston, MA: Beacon Press.

Tierney, R. (2010). Fairness in classroom assessment. In H. Andrade & G. Cizek (Eds.), *Handbook of formative assessment* (pp. 125–144). New York: Routledge.

Wiliam, D. (1992). Some technical issues in assessment: A user's guide. *British Journal of Curriculum and Assessment*, 2(3), 11–20.

Wiliam, D. (2010). An integrative summary of the research literature and implications for a new theory of formative assessment. In H. L. Andrade & G. J. Cizek (Eds.), *Handbook of formative assessment* (pp. 18–40). New York, NY: Routledge.

Zimmerman, B. J. (2002). Achieving self-regulation: The trial and triumph of adolescence. In F. Pajares & T. Urdan (Eds.), *Academic motivation of adolescents*. Greenwich, CT: Information Age Publishing.

Zimmerman, B. J., & Schunk, D. (Eds.). (2011). *Handbook of self-regulation of learning and performance*. New York, NY: Routledge.

2
Actionable Principles of Formative Assessment

Overview

Chapter 2 illustrates three key principles for effective implementation of formative assessment, each related to the three framing questions in Chapter 1. The principles include the integration of assessment into the process of teaching and learning, using assessment evidence to advance learning, and using assessment to support student self-regulation. Examples from elementary and middle school classrooms are used to show how the principles can be enacted.

Assessment is useful for informing ongoing teaching and learning when it provides a *prospective* view of learning in order to answer the question, "What is next for this student?" (Heritage, 2013a). As you can probably tell, it is this function of assessment that we find most compelling as educators. Why? Because effective formative assessment practice involves teachers and students in understanding where students currently are in their learning while they are still in the process of learning, and in making decisions about how to move that learning forward (Bell & Cowie, 2000; Heritage, 2010a, 2010b, 2013b; Swaffield, 2011). And as we saw in the example of Emily and Jason in Chapter 1, involving students in decisions about their own learning supports self-regulation.

Formative assessment is not an orthodoxy. It will likely look different in different teachers' classrooms and in different content areas. As Christine Harrison and Sally Howard observe, it is "consistency of principle" that matters in formative assessment, not "uniformity of practice" (2009, p. 32). In this chapter, we illustrate three key principles of practice for effective formative assessment, derived from the literature and verified from our firsthand knowledge of what occurs in classrooms:

> Principle 1: Assessment is integrated into the process of teaching and learning.
> Principle 2: Assessment evidence is used to move learning forward.
> Principle 3: Assessment supports student self-regulation.

Enacting these principles enables teachers and their students to answer the three framing questions of formative assessment that we introduced in Chapter 1: Where are we going? Where are we now? Where to next?

The process of teaching and learning is initiated and guided by the question: Where are we going? In other words, what are the goals of the lesson and how will we know if we have reached the goal? Opportunities to find out where students are in their learning (Where are we now?) arise during the learning process, both from teachers' planned strategies and from students' self-assessment. The evidence that emerges from these two sources is used to move learning forward, answering the third question: Where to next? In response to evidence, the teacher adjusts instruction or provides feedback to the students, which they use to improve their learning; the students also make decisions about their own learning tactics as a result of their internal feedback from self-assessment. In both instances, feedback is leveraged to support student self-regulation.

Next we will illustrate the three principles and three questions, first in the context of a middle school classroom, and then in a first-grade classroom.

Middle School Classroom

In this middle school classroom, students are learning to write persuasive essays. Ms. Roberts, the teacher, stands at the front of the class by the whiteboard, and the students are seated at desks close to her and to each other. Ms. Roberts begins by saying:

> So, you have been working on your essays. And one of the things I noticed when I was looking at your essays last night is . . . you guys have moves . . . you know something about essay writing. I was looking through all of your essays, and I was thinking about some of the things you know about how to make strong arguments.

She then turns to a large Post-it Note pasted on the whiteboard and on which she has written:

What we already know about strong arguments. . . .
- There is a strong claim.
- The claim has support (reasons).
- There is evidence for every reason.

- The essays should hook you, and set up the essay.
- There is a conclusion.
- There is some discussion of the counterclaim.

Ms. Roberts then goes over the list, providing information about each item. She tells the students that based on what she has seen from their current writing, they are ready to "lift the level of their essays up," that they have "got the foundation down," and that the purpose of today's lesson is to "build the building."

In the next part of the lesson, Ms. Roberts uses a "mentor" text—a long body paragraph that she has displayed so that the students can analyze what authors do, in her words, "to make strong arguments." After she reads the paragraph aloud, she asks the students to separate into small groups and discuss, "What is it about this part of an essay that makes it strong and persuasive?" While the students talk with each other, Ms. Roberts circulates, listening to the groups' conversations and intervening to probe what they are saying or to help them elaborate points.

Next, Ms. Roberts asks the students to come together as a whole group. She then leads a whole-class session to co-construct criteria for how they could make their own essays stronger and more developed, drawing from their previous discussions about the author's craft. When students offer their ideas, she consistently asks them to cite the basis for them in the text. As the students agree on the criteria, the teacher writes them on the whiteboard. At the end of the discussion, this is what she has written:

Ways we can develop our essays:
- Add specific/precise details.
- Choose the best, most persuasive evidence.

- Use tone to give voice to our essays.
- Connect how our evidence supports our reasons.

Ms. Roberts then invites the students to consider these criteria, "or anything else the author did to hers," in order to develop their essays further. After a period of reflection, the students exchange ideas with a partner about the current status of their essay and what each one is going to do, using some or all of the criteria, to strengthen his or her essay. Then they move to their own seats and continue with their essay writing.

Formative assessment takes place in the ongoing flow of activity and interactions in the classroom (Swaffield, 2011). It is not an adjunct to teaching, but rather is integrated into the process of teaching and learning (Principle 1). In this vignette, Ms. Roberts had examined students' first attempts at writing a persuasive essay and was able to determine what students knew about this genre of writing (Where are we now?), which she communicated to the students. Based on this evidence, she determined that the students were at a point where they could analyze author's craft in more detail and use what they learned to develop their own essays. While students discussed the mentor text, Ms. Roberts listened in to their discussions and interacted with the students, gaining insights into how students were thinking about the author's craft and offering teaching points along the way (Where are we now? Principle 1). In the large group session, she had a further source of evidence of students' thinking when she asked for ideas from their discussion and pressed them to cite the text to substantiate their points (Where are we now? Principle 2). In the last part of the lesson, Ms. Roberts asked the students to review their own writing and think about what they needed to do, relative to the criteria they had co-constructed, to develop their essays further (Where to next? Principle 3). They made their own decisions and, as a result, Ms. Roberts had another source of evidence to provide her with insights about how students were developing their understanding and application of author's craft (Principle 2 again). And because the students were clear about the goal and the criteria, they would be able to make an assessment of how well they had met the criteria, as well as being in a position to provide feedback to their peers about their work (Principle 3).

Elementary Mathematics Lesson

We will now consider the three formative assessment principles and questions in the context of Ms. Lewis' first-grade classroom (National Council of Teachers of Mathematics, 2014). In her previous lesson, Ms. Lewis observed that some students seemed unsure of the meaning of the equal sign as a symbol of equality, and she is concerned that other students may be uncertain about this as well (Where are we now? Principle 2). Based on this information, she planned a lesson with the goal of helping her students understand more clearly that the equal sign indicates that quantities or expressions "have the same value" (Where to next?).

Ms. Lewis begins the lesson by asking all the students to work on their own to solve the problem $8 + 4 = \_\_ + 7$. As the students work, she observes how they are solving the problem, makes notes about the different solutions and strategies the students are using, and probes some of the students' thinking to learn more about their reasoning (Where are we now? Principle 2). Ms. Lewis notices several different answers, including 12, 5, 19, 11, and 6, so she asks the students to find someone in the class with an answer that is different from their own to compare and discuss their solutions. She listens in to their discussion, noting that some students change their answers as a result of their conversations (Where to next? Principles 1 and 3).

After their discussions, Ms. Lewis asks the students to bring their papers to the rug so that they can discuss the work as a class. She asks Maddie to share her work first, which was the following:

8 + 4 = !2 + 7

OOOOOOOO + OOOO

Maddie explains that she didn't know what to do with the 7. The class agrees that the sum of 8 and 4 is 12, and they also agree that this fact seems to be an important thing to know in solving the problem.

Gabe presents his work next.

8 + 4 = 5 + 7

~~O~~ + O =   O
~~O~~   O   O
~~O~~   O   O
~~O~~   O   O
~~O~~   O
~~O~~   O
~~O~~   O
~~O~~

Gabe explains that he thought the total had to be the same on both sides of the equal sign, so he used his drawing to figure out that 5 will make both sides total 12. Ms. Lewis asks him to explain why he thought it might be true that both sides have to have the same total. He said that he thought about how they sometimes write equations that only have one number on the left, like 5 = 2 + 3, or when they write the "number of the day" in different ways without using an equal sign at all (for example, 12 as 4 + 4 + 4). The teacher asks the other students to comment on these ideas. Then Alex adds that they write the number of the day in different ways to name that number, and he suggests that this case might be something like that. Ms. Lewis asks all the students to turn and talk with a partner about how this problem might relate to their previous work when 12 was the number of the day.

After more whole-class discussion, Ms. Lewis asks all the students to return to their seats and take out a piece of paper. She asks them to make up a similar problem on their own and use it to complete this sentence starter: "The equal sign means that _____." The students find partners to review their work, and they make revisions based on their partners' feedback (Principle 3). Finally, she collects the students' work so she can do further analysis and determine the next steps in teaching and learning (Where to next? Principle 1).

As in the first vignette, assessment is fully integrated into instruction (Principle 1). Ms. Lewis has devised a learning experience for students that she can use as an assessment opportunity, particularly when she uses questions to probe students' reasoning (Where are we now?). She uses evidence from her previous observations of the students' work to plan the lesson, and she will also use the information she has obtained from the student discussions and their final work product to determine next steps (Where to next? Principle 2). Even though Ms. Lewis' students are first-graders, she involves them in assessment in ways that are appropriate for them: They review and discuss each other's work, provide feedback to each other, and then have the opportunity to revise their work before submitting it to Ms. Lewis (Where to next? Principle 3).

Diagnostic Items

Another effective way that the three principles can be enacted is through the use of carefully designed diagnostic items, which can take the form of questions or statements. For example, consider the following item, which a teacher could pose to students during a lesson on place value and then ask them to hold up their responses written on whiteboards:

Write two thousand sixty-seven as a number.

a) 267
b) 2067
c) 200067
d) 2000607

During a sequence of learning, diagnostic items can be a valuable means to provide insights into students' misconceptions. In the example above, the teacher can use the students' responses to determine which students do not understand that the correct answer is (b), and also to provide valuable diagnostic information about *how* students incorrectly think about place value (Ciofalo & Wylie, 2006). For example, a student who selected option (c) or option (d) is representing each number in the sentence by separating out the 2000 and then appending either 67 or first 60 and then 7, providing insight into how the student is thinking about place value. With this information, obtained during the course of teaching and learning (Where are we now? Principle 1), the teacher can take action intended to move learning forward (Where to next? Principle 2).

However, without inviting students to consider their responses based on her feedback, the teachers' use of the diagnostic item does not embrace Principle 3: Assessment supports student self-regulation. To enact Principle 3, the teacher could be very intentional about using the term "misconception," helping the students understand the purpose of the item and, through feedback, what their answers reveal about their misconceptions (C. Wylie, personal communication, May 2016). If the students are then asked to think about why they might have that misconception and set a goal for fixing it, Principle 3 would be addressed. One student's thoughts on the use of diagnostic items illustrates their value (Principle 3):

> *I feel that I can answer questions without being worried about getting it wrong. I can even explane [sic] my answer without being worried about it. I know if I get it wrong that I can just ask the teacher and that will help me improve my work because if I never know what I got wrong I will never learn the right way to do it.*
>
> (Wylie, Mawhinney, & Ciafolo, 2007, p. 9)

As you can see from the examples above, enacting Principle 1 (assessment is integrated into the process of teaching and learning) is a natural part of responsive, student-centered teaching. The examples illustrate just a few of the many ways that teachers and students can use formative assessment practices to deepen learning (Principle 2) and promote academic self-regulation (Principle 3).

Self-Regulated Learning, Self-Efficacy, and Motivation

In the preceding vignettes, we saw students being supported to develop self-regulated learning skills. In each classroom the students were generating their own ideas and taking action toward the attainment of their goals (Zimmerman, 2001), within a clear structural framework provided by their teachers. Additionally, two related factors impacting self-regulatory skills were being fostered: self-efficacy and motivation.

Self-efficacy refers to a person's belief in his or her capacity to perform actions that lead to a specific goal (Bandura, 1997; Schunk & Pajares, 2009; Wigfield, Eccles, Schiefele, Roeser, & Davis-Kean, 2006). For instance, students who have high self-efficacy regarding their math capabilities are more likely to persevere with challenging problems, ask for help in solving them, and tackle new math problems than students with low self-efficacy for math. In fact, students with low self-efficacy beliefs may decide they will not be successful even before they tackle the problem, and quickly give up. Self-efficacy is a foundation for motivation: Unless students believe that their actions can produce the results they desire, they have little incentive to act or persevere when faced with difficulties (Pajares, 2009).

Two additional motivational components contribute to the extent to which students engage in self-regulated learning: students' commitment to, and interest in, the learning goals, and their emotional reactions to the learning task (Pintrich & DeGroot, 1990). When students perceive little value in a task, they do not bring a goal-oriented perspective to their learning. As a result, they are much less motivated to engage in the learning, let alone self-regulation. When students' responses to the question "How do I feel about this task?" refer to feelings of anxiety or shame, for example, their capacity for self-regulation is diminished. In sum, self-regulated students display motivated actions: self-directed and self-controlled behaviors that are informed by metacognition (the awareness of one's own thinking) and propelled by a positive affective response to learning and the will to succeed (Paris & Paris, 2001).

Let us now return to the vignettes to see how self-efficacy beliefs and motivation are fostered and capitalized on in each classroom. In Ms. Roberts' class, students' feelings of self-efficacy are likely to be enhanced when she describes what they already know about essay writing and conveys to them that they have a strong foundation and are now ready to "lift the levels of their essays up." She uses a mentor text to develop criteria for how the students can further develop their writing, provoking a goal orientation and a manageable next step for their learning. Finally, the students are asked to engage in self-regulation by considering what they needed to do to their essays based on the criteria. The students' feelings of self-efficacy and motivation are enhanced through the agentive stance to their own learning that the teacher enables them to take.

Ms. Lewis also provides a context in which her first-grade students' feelings of self-efficacy can be enhanced. Her students solve problems, engage with each other to examine and discuss their solutions, and provide peer feedback. At no point in the vignette does she tell the students they are wrong. Instead she offers them several opportunities to advance their thinking with the support of herself and their peers. For example, the students revise their work based on their peers' feedback and, when they are working though their solutions, Ms. Lewis asks them to connect the current problem to previous work, assisting them to recognize that they are building on prior learning.

In the case of the example of the diagnostic item, one student clearly underscored her emotional reaction to the task and her feelings of self-efficacy: *I feel that I can answer questions without being worried about getting it wrong.* While research suggests that young children can have overly optimistic self-efficacy beliefs, a troubling finding is that as students get older they become less confident in their capabilities to accomplish challenging goals and to regulate their learning in accomplishing them (Wigfield, Klauda, & Cambria, 2011). When the three assessment principles outlined above are effectively enacted in the classroom, and students and teachers collaborate, as we saw in the vignettes, to answer the three framing questions of formative assessment, feelings of self-efficacy can be fostered, motivation can be boosted, and self-regulatory skills are supported for all students.

In the next chapter, we focus on learning goals and success criteria, which help students and their teachers answer the question "Where are we going?" This is an essential question for enacting the three principles and providing the goal orientation for self-regulation.

References

Bandura, A. (1997). *Self-efficacy: The exercise of control.* New York, NY: W. H. Freeman.

Bell, B., & Cowie, B. (2000). The characteristics of formative assessment in science education. *Science Education, 85,* 536–553.

Ciofalo, J. F., & Wylie, E. C. (2006). Using diagnostic classroom assessment: One question at a time. *TCRecord.* Retrieved from www.tcrecord.org. ID Number: 12285.

Harrison, C., & Howard, S. (2009). *Inside the primary black box: Assessment for learning in primary and early years classrooms.* London, UK: GL Assessment.

Heritage, M. (2010a). *Formative assessment: Making it happen in the classroom.* Thousand Oaks, CA: Corwin Press.

Heritage, M. (2010b). *Formative assessment and next-generation assessment systems: Are we losing an opportunity?* Paper commissioned by The Council of Chief State School Officers, Washington, DC.

Heritage, M. (2013a). Gathering evidence of student understanding. In J. H. McMillan (Ed.), *SAGE handbook of research on classroom assessment* (pp. 179–193). New York. SAGE.

Heritage, M. (2013b). *Formative assessment: A process of inquiry and action.* Cambridge, MA: Harvard Education Press.

National Council of Teachers of Mathematics. (2014). *Principles into actions*. Reston, VA: Author.

Pajares, F. (2009). *Sources of self-efficacy beliefs*. Retrieved from www.education.com/reference/article/self-efficacy-theory/#A

Paris, S. G., & Paris, A. H. (2001). Classroom applications of research on self-regulated learning. *Educational Psychologist, 36*(2), 89–101.

Pintrich, P. R., & DeGroot, E. (1990). *Quantitative and qualitative perspectives on student motivational beliefs and self-regulated learning*. Paper presented at the annual meeting of the American Educational Research Association, Boston, MA.

Schunk, D. H., & Pajares, F. (2009). Self-efficacy theory. In K. Wentzel, A. Wigfield, & D. Miele (Eds.), *Handbook of motivation at school* (pp. 35–53). Abingdon: Routledge.

Swaffield, S. (2011). Getting to the heart of authentic assessment for learning. *Assessment in Education: Principles, Policy and Practice, 18*(4), 433–449.

The Teachers College Reading and Writing Project. (n.d.) *Teaching Students to Examine Craft Moves and Author's Intent in Mentor Persuasive Essay in Order to Support Revision*. Retrieved from http://readingandwritingproject.org/resources/units-of-study-implementation/units-of-study-classroom-videos#

Wigfield, A., Eccles, J. S., Schiefele, U., Roeser, R., & Davis-Kean, P. (2006). Development of achievement motivation. In W. Damon & N. Eisenberg (Eds.), *Handbook of child psychology* (Vol. 3, pp. 933–1002). New York: Wiley.

Wigfield, A., Klauda, S. L., & Cambria, J. (2011). Influences on the development of academic self-regulatory processes. *Handbook of self-regulation of learning and performance* (pp. 33–48). New York: Wiley.

Wylie, C., Mawhinney, L., & Ciofalo, J. (2007). *Diagnostic questions*. Paper presentation at the annual meeting of the American Educational Research Association, Chicago, IL.

Zimmerman, B. J. (2001). Theories of self-regulated learning and academic achievement: An overview and analysis. In B. J. Zimmerman & D. H. Schunk (Eds.), *Self-regulated learning and academic achievement: Theoretical perspectives* (2nd ed., pp. 1–37). Mahwah, NJ: Erlbaum.

3
Clear Learning Goals and Criteria

Overview

The focus of this chapter is on how learning goals and success criteria are used by teachers and students to know "Where are we going?" The chapter shows how to derive goals from standards, how to establish performance and product criteria using checklists and rubrics, and how goals and criteria are used to promote self-regulation. The final section of the chapter shows how to co-construct criteria with students.

Articulating clear goals and criteria for learning helps teachers and students answer the question, "Where are we going?" Variously called learning intentions, learning goals, and learning targets, goals describe the skills, concepts, analytical practices, and dispositions that constitute the intended consequences of teaching and learning (Andrade & Brookhart, 2016; Heritage, Walqui, & Linquanti, 2015). For example, in Chapter 1, the learning goal for Jason and Emily's students was to apply their knowledge about the nature of gradation to their drawings. In Chapter 2, the first-grade students' math learning goal was to understand that the equal sign indicates that quantities or expressions have the same value. In Figure 1.2 in Chapter 1, the setting of goals by a teacher is step A, and goal setting by the student is step C.

Hattie (2009) defines effective goal setting by teachers as setting appropriately challenging goals, developing commitment on the part of teachers and students to attain them, and implementing strategies to achieve them. When goals are determined by the teacher, it is necessary to share them with students, who can use them to begin to answer the question, "Where am I going?" It can make a difference. For example, Seidel, Rimmele, and Prenzel (2005) found a positive effect of physics teachers' goal clarity and coherence on students' motivation and perceptions of supportive learning conditions, as well as big improvements in scores on tests on electric circuits and force.

Learning goals should not be thought of as discrete but rather as part of a continuum leading to deeper learning. The middle school writing vignette in Chapter 2 is an example of how this works. The lesson described in the vignette is part of an extended sequence of lessons: The students were building on what they had already learned and, in subsequent lessons, would continue to incrementally develop their knowledge of authors' craft in their essay writing.

Learning Goals Derived From Standards

Ultimately, the goal of learning is achievement of standards that specify what students need to learn, usually by the end of each grade level or band of grade levels. How well students have achieved the standards is determined, in large part, by the annual assessments that states require students to take. The purpose of formative assessment is to help teachers and students keep learning on track toward meeting the standards, day by day. Consequently, learning goals as we envision them are short term, at the lesson level (one or more class periods). When taken together, they provide the pathway for students to move incrementally to achieving the standards.

To derive lesson-sized learning goals from standards, teachers need to consider several factors. We will illustrate these factors with one of the fourth-grade Common Core mathematics standards (Formative Assessment Insights, 2015):

> 4.NF.1: Explain why a fraction a/b is equivalent to a fraction $(n \times a)/(n \times b)$ by using visual fraction models, with attention to how the number and size of the parts differ even though the two fractions themselves are the same size. Use this principle to recognize and generate equivalent fractions.

When teachers are planning learning goals from this standard, they first need to consider the relevant prior knowledge that students are building on from the third-grade standards, in this case:

> 3.NF.1 Understand a fraction $1/b$ as the quantity formed by 1 part when a whole is partitioned into b equal parts; understand a fraction a/b as the quantity formed by a parts of size $1/b$.
>
> 3.NF.2 Understand a fraction as a number on the number line; represent fractions on a number line diagram.
>
> 3.NF.3 Explain equivalence of fractions in special cases, and compare fractions by reasoning about their size.

Working from the third-grade standards, teachers consider the building blocks—the incremental changes in student thinking about fractions that occur as they move toward meeting the fourth-grade standard. Some of these might include: understanding that fractions are equivalent if they are the same size in an area model or they label the same point on a number line; recognizing and generating simple equivalent fractions and explaining why they are equivalent; writing whole numbers as fractions and recognizing fractions that are equal to whole numbers, and so on. Once teachers have identified the building blocks as a continuum that makes sense in terms of the development of students' thinking, they are able to derive lesson-learning goals. Importantly, the goals of each lesson will be connected to what came before and where students are going next, which is essential if students are going to reach deeper levels of learning.

In addition to creating building blocks, it is also helpful to decide on potential challenges that students may experience as their thinking develops. For example, students may use different sized wholes when drawing area models, which may lead to incorrect representations and/or comparisons of the sizes of different fractions. Not only will this information help teachers plan instruction, as we shall see in Chapter 4, it will also be useful for interpreting students' thinking from the planned evidence gathering during a lesson.

The preceding example from a fourth-grade unit on fractions demonstrates the importance of a deep understanding of standards in setting the foundation on which the building blocks rest. (For standards related to dance, music, theater, visual arts, and moving image, see the New York City Department of Education's *Blueprints for Teaching and Learning in the Arts*: http://schools.nyc.gov/offices/teachlearn/arts/blueprints.html).

> **Text Box 3.1   Guidelines for Learning Goals**
>
> - Connected to the big picture of learning (e.g., standards)
> - Focused on learning (e.g., we are learning to . . .)
> - Lead to deeper learning and transferable skills and practices
> - Are realistic and manageable in limited time (e.g., a lesson)
> - Shared with and understood by students (i.e., in age-appropriate language, clarified and discussed with students at the beginning of the instructional sequence or unit)

Learning Goals Derived From Learning Progressions

Meeting college and career ready standards is the ultimate academic goal for students in grades K–12. Standards are descriptions of knowledge, skills, and understandings to be learned by the end of a particular period of time, usually by the end of specific grade levels. End-of-year assessments are aligned to standards and provide summative information about students' achievement within particular grade levels. However, because standards do not describe the intermediate pathways of between one grade-level's standards and the next, they do not represent the level of detail needed for formative assessment and instruction.

A further limitation of standards for formative assessment is that they do not illuminate how partial or naïve understandings might present themselves. Partial or naïve understandings are a prime concern in formative assessment; teachers need to understand what these are in order to move students to more complete understandings (Wylie, Bauer, Bailey, & Heritage, in press). For these reasons, there has been significant interest, from a variety of disciplines, in learning progressions (Bailey & Heritage, 2014; Heritage, 2008; Sztajn, Confrey, Wilson, & Edgington, 2012).

Also known as learning trajectories, construct maps, or construct models, a learning progression is a model of successively more sophisticated ways of thinking about a topic (National Research Council, 2007). Unlike end-of-grade level standards, progressions are not prescriptive, but instead convey a sequence of "expected tendencies" in student learning along a continuum of developing expertise (Confrey & Maloney, 2010). In general, progressions are based on research about how students' learning actually advances, as opposed to selecting sequences of topics and learning experiences based only on logical analysis of current disciplinary knowledge, which is more the case in standards development. Researchers develop hypotheses, which are then tested empirically to ensure construct validity (Corcoran, Mosher, & Rogat, 2009).

Detailed descriptions of typical learning serve as representations of models of cognition that can inform instruction as well as the design and interpretation of assessment information. As is shown in Figure 3.1, learning progressions can also indicate common pre- and misconceptions students have about a topic.

Learning progressions provide a blueprint for instruction and assessment because they represent a goal for summative assessment, indicate a sequence of activities for instruction, and can inform the design of formative assessment processes that provide indicators of students' understanding (Corcoran et al., 2009; Songer, Kelcey, & Gotwals, 2009). Teachers and districts can design summative assessments with a learning progression in mind, as well as formative

4	Student is able to coordinate apparent and actual motion of objects in the sky. Student knows that: • the Earth is both orbiting the Sun and rotating on its axis • the Earth orbits the Sun once per year • the Earth rotates on its axis once per day, causing the day/night cycle and the appearance that the Sun moves across the sky • the Moon orbits the Earth once every 28 days, producing the phases of the Moon COMMON ERROR: Seasons are caused by the changing distance between the Earth and Sun. COMMON ERROR: The phases of the Moon are caused by a shadow of the planets, the Sun, or the Earth falling on the Moon.
3	Student knows that: • the Earth orbits the Sun • the Moon orbits the Earth • the Earth rotates on its axis However, student has not put this knowledge together with an understanding of apparent motion to form explanations and may not recognize that the Earth is both rotating and orbiting simultaneously. COMMON ERROR: It gets dark at night because the Earth goes around the Sun once a day.
2	Student recognizes that: • the Sun appears to move across the sky every day • the observable shape of the Moon changes every 28 days • Student may believe that the Sun moves around the Earth. COMMON ERROR: All motion in the sky is due to the Earth spinning on its axis. COMMON ERROR: The Sun travels around the Earth. COMMON ERROR: It gets dark at night because the Sun goes around the Earth once a day. COMMON ERROR: The Earth is the center of the universe.
1	Student does not recognize the systematic nature of the appearance of objects in the sky. Student may not recognize that the Earth is spherical. COMMON ERROR: It gets dark at night because something (e.g., clouds, the atmosphere, "darkness") covers the Sun. COMMON ERROR: The phases of the Moon are caused by clouds covering the Moon. COMMON ERROR: The Sun goes below the Earth at night.

Figure 3.1 Scoring Rubric from *Construct Map for Student Understanding of Earth in the Solar System*

Adapted from Briggs, Alonzo, Schwab, & Wilson (2006)

assessments that move learning ahead (e.g., see Furtak & Heredia, 2014). Questions that target common misconceptions can be designed in advance and delivered verbally, in writing, to individuals, or to groups. For example, at a particular point in a unit on Earth and the solar system, a teacher can ask questions designed to reveal student thinking in relation to a specific learning goal in a progression, such as "How long does it take the Earth to go around the Sun, and how do you know?" The students' responses to the questions provide insight into their learning, and can guide the teacher's next pedagogical steps.

Diagnostic questions can also be implemented in the form of multiple-choice items (Ciofalo & Wylie, 2006; Wylie, Ciofalo, & Mavronikolas, 2010). Briggs et al. (2006) have demonstrated that multiple-choice items based on construct maps, a.k.a. learning progressions, can provide diagnostic information to teachers about student understanding. When each of the possible answer choices in an item is linked to developmental levels of student understanding, as in the example in Figure 3.2, an item-level analysis of student responses can reveal what individual students and the class as a whole understand.

Which is the best explanation for why it gets dark at night?
  A. The Moon blocks the Sun at night. [Level 1 response]
  B. The Earth rotates on its axis once a day. [Level 4 response]
  C. The Sun moves around the Earth once a day. [Level 2 response]
  D. The Earth moves around the Sun once a day. [Level 3 response]
  E. The Sun and Moon switch places to create night. [Level 2 response]

Figure 3.2 Diagnostic Item Based on *Construct Map for Student Understanding of Earth in the Solar System*

Source: Briggs et al. (2006)

For example, if one quarter of the students in a class choose option D, which suggests that they believe that darkness is caused by the Earth moving around the Sun once a day, the teacher might decide to provide opportunities for structured small group discussions between students who do and do not understand the day-night cycle. More intensive interventions can be implemented for the portion of the class who scored at level 2 or below by selecting options A, C, or E.

Briggs et al. (2006) note that, while diagnostic items based on a model of cognition represent an improvement over tests consisting of traditional multiple-choice items, they complement but do not replace rich, open-ended performance tasks. However, recent evidence suggests that such items are actually better than open-ended items at eliciting responses similar to the understanding that students express in think-alouds and interviews, perhaps because the items probe students' understanding by offering plausible response alternatives (Steedle & Shavelson, 2009).

Performance and Product Criteria

Criteria for students' performances should be well aligned to the learning goals in order to address the question, "Where are we going?" Criteria provide indicators to teachers and students about what meeting the learning goals entails. In other words, criteria help them recognize if learning is successful or not. For example, in Chapter 2, the students and teacher co-constructed the criteria for making their essays strong and persuasive, and then considered which criteria they needed to use to further develop their own writing. In Chapter 1, the art students co-constructed criteria for gradation, based on the visual rubric provided by their teacher. In both examples, students had opportunities to understand "what counts," as they sometimes put it, or "what successful learning looks like," as we like to say.

Criteria are more specific than learning goals, and can relate to either a performance or a product. Performance criteria specify what learners should be able to say, do, make, or write in order to indicate success in learning (cf. Griffin, 2009). Product criteria are even more specific: They articulate the qualities or characteristics of student work on a particular task that indicate achievement of the learning goals. Although performance criteria can stand on their own, when they are used to create product criteria for rubrics or checklists, the learning goals and assessment tools are bridged, like so:

> Learning goals → Performance criteria → Product criteria (as needed) → Rubric or checklist

Figure 3.3 is an example of how specificity increases as we move from learning goals to performance criteria to product criteria. The learning goal for this seventh-grade mathematics class was to use the Pythagorean Theorem to find the length of the hypotenuse, or a leg of a right triangle. The performance criteria are items one through six: understand the task, explain what is known, and so on. The product criteria are listed in the checklist under item six, check the solution: appropriate formula, diagram, work is shown, etc. (Andrade & Warner, 2012).

Performance Criteria

Performance criteria specify what learners should be able to say, do, make, or write to indicate success in learning.

1	**Understand the task**	I can clearly state what the problem is asking me to find.
2	**Explain what is known**	I can clearly explain the given information (what I know from the problem). I use words, numbers, and diagrams as appropriate.
3	**Plan an approach**	I can clearly describe my chosen strategy, which is efficient and sophisticated (e.g., "I will make a table," "I will make an organized list," or "I will draw a diagram").
4	**Solve the problem**	I use my plan to solve every part of the problem. If my strategy doesn't work, I try a new one. I write out all the steps in my solution so the reader doesn't have to guess at how or why I did what I did. I use words, numbers, and diagrams/charts/graphs, as appropriate. My work is clearly labeled.
5	**Explain the solution**	I clearly explain my solution and why I believe it is correct using precise and correct math terms and notations. I check to make sure my solution is reasonable. I check for possible flaws in my reasoning or my computations. If I can, I solve the problem in a different way and get the same answer.
6	**Check the solution**	I check my solution according to the **product criteria**: _____ Appropriate formula or let statement _____ Diagram with clear labels (if appropriate) _____ All work shown and connected to final answer _____ Correct calculations and order of operations _____ Final answer clearly identified _____ Answer labeled with units (if appropriate) _____ Answer correctly rounded to the requested decimal place (if appropriate) If my solution is incorrect, I find my mistake, determine a new plan, solve the problem, and justify my new answer.

Figure 3.3 Performance and Product Criteria for Seventh-Grade Mathematics Unit on the Pythagorean Theorem

Source: Andrade & Warner (2012)

For example, in a third-grade math class the learning goal for the students was:

> Today we are learning to use multiplication and division to solve problems.

The performance criteria were:

- I can determine when and how to break a problem into simpler parts.
- I can explain what the problem is asking me to do.
- I can explain the relationship between multiplication and division.

Before the students began to solve the problem, the teacher spent time discussing the goal with the students, reminding them that this lesson was part of a sequence focused on problem solving, and unpacking with them the meaning of the criteria. The class spent extended time discussing the relationship between multiplication and division. While the students focused on a specific problem in this lesson, the criteria were generalizable to similar problems. As a result, the students could internalize these criteria and apply them to other problems they encounter.

The next example shows the learning goal and performance criteria for a seventh-grade integrated English language development lesson. The lesson focuses on using cross-cutting language functions in the context of reading a secondary source text.

As in the math example, the teacher discussed the goal and criteria with the students, using a secondary source text to model the performance criteria. In particular, the teacher clarified the language of description and explanation. In this way, the students had a conception of what

> **Text Box 3.2 English Language Performance Criteria**
>
> Learning goal: Critique the perspective of a secondary source text about the Spanish conquistadors' exploration of Mexico.
>
> **Performance Criteria**
>
> - Describe the historical event.
> - Identify the perspective from which the text is written and explain how I know that.
> - Explain which perspectives are missing and why I think that.

meeting the learning goal entailed in terms of text analysis and language use.

Product Criteria

Product criteria further specify the learning goals by describing the qualities of student work on a particular assignment that demonstrate a successful performance. Product criteria can be communicated to students in a variety of ways, including models/exemplars, worked examples, rubrics, and checklists. Models and worked examples, which typically consist of a sample problem and the appropriate steps to its solution, imply success criteria (Hattie, 2009). Worked examples can provide students with correct and incorrect answers, along with questions that encourage students to explain the problem back to themselves, thereby identifying the criteria for effective problem solving (e.g., Booth, Lange, Koedinger, & Newton, 2013).

Checklists

Product criteria can be explicitly communicated through high-quality rubrics and checklists. A checklist is just a list of criteria, without the descriptions of levels of quality found in a rubric. Checklists are useful when a characteristic of student work is either present or absent (no gray areas in terms of quality, which is rare), or when students are young and/or preliterate and cannot decode a lot of text.

Figure 3.4 is a checklist used by a teacher of kindergarten students with very limited literacy experience. At the beginning of the school year, Liliana DiGiorno realized that her new students did not know that writing was done from left to right and top to bottom of a page. Some of them were not aware that the marks they were making

Kindergarten Self-Checklist

_____	👄	Does my writing make sense?
_____	x⟶ ⇒	Did I start writing on the left side of the page?
_____	✏️	Is my writing neat?
_____	ABC	Did I start my sentences with an uppercase letter?
_____	👁	Did I write words the way I learned them?
_____	. ? !	Did I use punctuation?

Figure 3.4 Kindergarten Writing Checklist

Source: Liliana DiGiorno (personal communication)

on paper were intended to be read. Using this information, Ms. DiGiorno asked her school's art teachers to draw symbols to represent beginning product criteria for her students' writing, for example, the mouth graphic meant the words make sense when spoken, and the image of an eye referred to sight words written on the board. Her use of information about students' needs reflects Principle 2: Assessment evidence is used to move learning forward.

Once the students learned the meaning of the symbols on the checklist, they were asked to check their writing as they worked. This is an example of Principle 3 in action: Assessment supports student self-regulation. Ms. DiGiorno was struck by the fact that the children began to closely attend to their work. They were eager to check off each item on the list and to revise their writing when they found a problem. Children who previously seemed to pay no attention to the quality of their work and to resist redoing anything now revised so strenuously that they erased holes into their papers—an unintended consequence of enacting Principle 3 through self-assessment in kindergarten. Ms. DiGiorno added a mini-lesson on gentle erasing (Principle 2 again).

The students also learned about punctuation, a concept that Ms. DiGiorno expected to have to leave to the first-grade teacher. When her students saw it on the list, however, they demanded to know what it was and how to do it: You get what you assess.

Rubrics

A rubric is a coherent set of criteria for students' work that includes descriptions of levels of performance quality on each criterion (Brookhart, 2013). Rubrics can be thought of as checklists with levels. Figure 1.1 (p. 6) and Figure 3.5

are both rubrics because they contain criteria and descriptive levels.

High-quality rubrics are closely aligned with the learning goals and performance criteria. The rubrics that are most useful to students are those that not only describe high-quality work but also flag common pitfalls to avoid, such as using the same words over and over and over (for example, see the persuasive essay rubric in Figure 3.5). Rubrics that communicate the standards of the discipline and warn about challenges that many students encounter can teach as well as assess.

Handing a rubric to students might help them learn—or it might not. A study that looked at the effect of simply providing a rubric to eighth-grade students before they began to write showed that, of three essays, only one resulted in significant differences between the treatment and comparison groups (Andrade, 2001). Because learning is a consequence of thinking (Perkins, 1992), students must actively think about and with the content of a rubric—not just wait to see how their teacher uses it to grade their assignments. An amusing anecdote related to that simple fact occurred when Heidi and her colleague (Andrade & Warner, 2012) implemented self-assessment in the seventh-grade mathematics classroom referenced in this chapter (see Figure 3.3). The teacher of that math class, Corrine Vinehout, had introduced the learning goals, the performance criteria, and the product criteria to her students many times over the course of the unit. Nonetheless, when she had them actually use the checklist to self-assess and correct their own solutions to extended-response problems, one student exclaimed, "So *this* is how you score our work!" Ms. Vinehout was incredulous: She reminded him that they had been over this material before, to which another student replied, "Yeah, but now we really get it."

The students knew what research has confirmed: Simply being told about goals and criteria is not enough—learners need to intellectually engage with them in order to really get it. In fact, studies have shown that when students are meaningfully engaged in co-creating and using rubrics to assess their own work, they tend to learn more, produce higher-quality assignments, and even become better at self-regulated learning (Brown & Harris, 2013; Panadero & Romero, 2014).

Heidi and her colleagues (Andrade, Du, & Mycek, 2010; Andrade, Du, & Wang, 2008) also used rubrics to communicate product criteria to the elementary and middle school students in their studies of formative self-assessment of writing. Students read a model essay, discussed its qualities, and generated a list of criteria that were then included in the rubric they used to self-assess drafts of their own essays (see Figure 3.5 for an example). Then students revised, of course—there is no point in self-assessment without revision. Scores for the treatment group's essays were practically and statistically higher than those of the comparison group, which suggests that assessing their own work in terms of the product criteria helped students identify paths to improvement. As they put it, their rubric-referenced self-assessments help them see "what I need to work on." And, for the most part, they do work on making improvements.

Ross and Starling (2008) also ensured that the ninth-grade geography students in their study understood and could apply the criteria for assessment to their own work. Before they self-assessed their projects, students were involved in defining assessment criteria by co-constructing a rubric. They then learned to apply the criteria through teacher modeling.

After controlling for the effects of self-efficacy, students in the self-assessment group scored higher than students

	4	3	2	1
Ideas and Content	The topic is focused and the main thesis is clear. Relevant, accurate facts and details provide evidence for the thesis. The author explains how the facts support the thesis, and addresses opposing views.	The topic is evident but broad and lacking in detail. The writing stays on topic but doesn't address minor parts of the assignment.	There is a very general topic but the writing strays off topic or doesn't address major parts of the assignment.	The topic and main ideas are unclear. The writing may be repetitious or disconnected thoughts with no main point.
Organization	The essay has an interesting motivator, developed middle, and scintillating conclusion that restates the thesis in new ways. The middle paragraphs each have a topic sentence and concluding sentence. The order of ideas makes sense.	The paper has a beginning, middle, and end. Sequencing is logical.	The paper has an attempt at an introduction and/or conclusion. Some ideas seem out of order.	There is no real introduction or conclusion. Ideas seem strung together in a loose fashion.

Figure 3.5 Seventh-Grade Persuasive Essay Rubric

Source: Andrade et al. (2010)

Voice	The writing matches the purpose and audience. The author seems to care about the topic. Tone and style are engaging.	The writing seems sincere but the author's voice fades in and out.	The writer seems to be aware of an audience but does not attempt to engage it.	The writing is inappropriate for the purpose or audience, and bland or mechanical.
Word Choice	Uses specific, powerful words, striking phrases, and lively verbs.	Words used are adequate, with a few attempts at powerful language.	Words used are ordinary but generally correct.	Limited, repetitive vocabulary. Some words used incorrectly.
Sentence Fluency	Sentences are well constructed and have different beginnings and lengths. Easy to read aloud.	Sentences are usually correct. Some variety in beginnings and length.	Many poorly constructed sentences. Little variety in beginnings/length.	The paper is hard to read because of incomplete, run-on, and awkward sentences.
Conventions	Double spaced. Few errors in spelling, punctuation, capitalization, grammar. Uses third person.	Conventions are usually correct. Some problems with grammar, syntax, and/or paragraphing.	Errors are frequent enough to be distracting.	Frequent errors make the paper difficult to read.

Figure 3.5 Continued

in the comparison group on all of the achievement measures, which included a Global Information System map, a report, and an exam (Ross & Starling, 2008). Here again, it appears that high-level cognitive engagement via the co-construction of criteria and careful self-assessment is related to learning and achievement. In Chapter 4 we will examine how peer assessment (perhaps better named peer feedback) can have very similar effects.

Recent reviews of rubrics as formative assessment tools are encouraging. Brookhart and Chen's (2014) review of studies of the use of rubrics suggested that the association between rubrics and students' academic performance and motivation was positive overall. They claim that rubrics can provide useful information if certain conditions are met, most notably the inclusion of clear, focused criteria. Panadero and Jonsson (2013) looked at 21 studies of rubrics and concluded that, used formatively, rubrics can support learning by increasing the transparency of teacher expectations, reducing anxiety, aiding the feedback process, improving student self-efficacy, and/or supporting student self-regulation.

Text Box 3.3 Guidelines for Criteria

- Clearly aligned to the learning goal
- Focused on learning
- Specify performance and/or product criteria
- Understood by students (in age-appropriate language, clarified and discussed with students, or co-constructed with students)
- Used by students to monitor their learning

Goals, Criteria, and Self-Regulation

Students' understandings of their teachers' goals and criteria can influence their regulation of their learning (Andrade & Brookhart, 2016). For example, a student who interprets a reading assignment as a memorization task will plan to use low-level cognitive processes and consider herself successful once key terms are memorized. In contrast, a student who interprets the same assignment as requiring understanding the central idea of the text will employ sophisticated comprehension strategies (assuming she knows them) and define success as being able to explain the main idea and how it is conveyed through particular details in the text.

Teachers cannot assume that criteria will be uniformly adopted and applied by students: Efforts must be made to ensure accurate and effective interpretations of the criteria (Butler & Cartier, 2004) and the learning goals. When students have a true understanding of the learning goals and criteria, they can do what highly self-regulated learners do: accurately assess their learning as it is developing, and then take action in order to close the gap between their current learning and the goal (Hattie & Timperley, 2007; Sadler, 1989).

Co-Constructing Criteria With Students

We have emphasized the need for meaningful, thought-provoking engagement with goals and criteria if students are to understand, internalize, and apply them. We have used the term *co-construction* in that context several times; but what does it really mean? It is important to be clear about this since, at its worst, co-constructing criteria can result in idiosyncratic, incoherent lists of qualities that differ from class to class and have no obvious connection to the standards of the discipline. This is a fear that principals occasionally confess to harboring—and with good reason.

Fortunately, most teachers understand their role in co-constructing criteria. The *co-* in *co-construction* means that the teachers have had a hand in determining criteria—they do not just step aside while students do it. Most teachers also know about the value of sharing exemplars or models before asking students to generate criteria by describing the characteristics of the models that demonstrate deep learning. This is what Ms. Roberts did in Chapter 2, when she had her fourth-graders analyze a mentor text in terms of its persuasiveness. Many teachers also share examples that illustrate difficulties that learners often encounter in order to help them avoid typical problems. Mr. Rondinelli and Ms. Maddy did so by sharing the visual gradation rubric with their students.

Analyzing examples such as mentor texts and worked mathematical problems and then brainstorming a list of characteristics that describe quality is probably the most common approach to co-constructing criteria. Because this approach is grounded in exemplary work and guided by an expert in the discipline (the teacher), the results differ little from class to class. Just as a rose is a rose is a rose, good writing is good writing, good problem solving is good problem solving, good analysis is good analysis, and so on. The criteria generated by particular groups of students tend to differ only in terms of word choices, not underlying meaning.

So why bother at all, if you know, more or less, where you will end up? Because analyzing models and co-constructing criteria involve meaningful, thought-provoking engagement that leads to learning. Simply handing out a list of criteria might seem to be more efficient, but students do not learn much that way. In our experience, the 30 to 40 minutes spent co-creating product criteria for a new project is well worth it.

Some teachers co-construct entire rubrics with their students—criteria, levels of quality, and all—which is impressive but perhaps unnecessary. Heidi, a relatively hard-core enthusiast of co-construction, never co-creates an entire rubric anymore. She always co-creates *criteria* for new, unfamiliar assignments, but wordsmithing a whole rubric is tedious and takes too much time. If it seemed to have additional benefits beyond what the process of co-constructing criteria has to offer, she might make time; but often it does not. Generating a list of characteristics as a class that can later be synthesized into a shorter list of criteria provides enough instructional leverage. The descriptive levels of a rubric can usually be written by the teacher, on her own time, without a loss of student learning.

Learning goals and criteria are the drivers of formative assessment because they answer the question, "Where am I going?" Goals and criteria function as an interpretive framework for teachers to determine where students are in their learning and what comes next, and for students to monitor their own learning and take action when they perceive discrepancies between their current learning and the goal (Principle 3: Assessment supports student self-regulation). Chapter 4 addresses the next step: collecting and interpreting evidence to answer the question, "Where are they (or am I) now?"

References

Andrade, H. G. (2001). The effects of instructional rubrics on learning to write. *Current Issues in Education*, *4*(4). Retrieved from http://cie.ed.asu.edu/volume4/number4.

Andrade, H., & Brookhart, S. M. (2016). The role of classroom assessment in supporting self-regulated learning. In D. Laveault & L. Allal (Eds.), *Assessment for learning: Meeting the challenge of implementation* (pp. 293–309). Heidelberg: Springer.

Andrade, H., Du, Y., & Mycek, K. (2010). Rubric-referenced self-assessment and middle school students' writing. *Assessment in Education, 17*(2), 199–214.

Andrade, H., Du, Y., & Wang, X. (2008). Putting rubrics to the test: The effect of a model, criteria generation, and rubric-referenced self-assessment on elementary school students' writing. *Educational Measurement: Issues and Practices, 27*(2), 3–13.

Andrade, H., & Warner, Z. (2012). Beyond "I give myself an A": Meaningful, rubric-referenced student self-assessment. *Educator's Voice, V*(42), 42–51.

Bailey, A. L., & Heritage, M. (2014). The role of language learning progressions in improved instruction and assessment of English language learners. *TESOL Quarterly, 48*(3), 480–506.

Booth, J. L., Lange, K. E., Koedinger, K. R., & Newton, K. J. (2013). Example problems that improve student learning in algebra: Differentiating between correct and incorrect examples. *Learning and Instruction, 25*, 24–34.

Briggs, D. C., Alonzo, A. C., Schwab, C., & Wilson, M. (2006). Diagnostic assessment with ordered multiple choice items. *Educational Assessment, 11*(1), 33–63.

Brookhart, S. M. (2013). *How to create and use rubrics for formative assessment and grading*. Alexandria, VA: ASCD.

Brookhart, S., & Chen, F. (2014). The quality and effectiveness of descriptive rubrics. *Educational Review, 67*(3), 343–368. doi:10.1080/00131911.2014.929565

Brown, G. T., & Harris, L. R. (2013). Student self-assessment. In J. H. McMillan (Ed.), *SAGE handbook of research on classroom assessment* (pp. 367–393). Thousand Oaks, CA: SAGE.

Butler, D. L., & Cartier, S. (2004). Promoting students' active and productive interpretation of academic work: A key to successful teaching and learning. *Teachers College Record, 106*(9), 1729–1758.

Ciofalo, J. F., & Wylie, E. C. (2006). Using diagnostic classroom assessment: One question at a time. *TCRecord*. Date published: January 10, 2006. http://www.tcrecord.org. ID Number: 12285.

Confrey, J., & Maloney, A. (June 2010). *The construction, refinement, and early validation of the equipartitioning learning trajectory*. Proceedings of the 9th International Conference of the Learning Sciences-Volume 1 (pp. 968–975). International Society of the Learning Sciences.

Corcoran, T. B., Mosher, F. A., & Rogat, A. (2009). Learning progressions in science: An evidence-based approach to reform. *CPRE Research Reports*. Retrieved from http://repository.upenn.edu/cpre_researchreports/53

Formative Assessment Insights. (2015). *Online digital learning experience*. San Francisco, CA: WestEd.

Furtak, E. M., & Heredia, S. C. (2014). Exploring the influence of learning progressions in two teacher communities. *Journal of Research in Science Teaching, 51*(8), 982–1020.

Griffin, P. (2009). Teachers' use of assessment data. In C. Wyatt-Smith & J. Cumming (Eds.), *Educational assessment in the 21st century* (pp. 183–208). Rotterdam, the Netherlands: Springer.

Hattie, J. (2009). *Visible learning: A synthesis of over 800 meta-analyses relating to achievement*. Oxford, UK: Routledge.

Hattie, J., & Timperley, H. (2007). The power of feedback. *Review of Educational Research, 77*, 81–112.

Heritage, M. (2008). *Learning progressions: Supporting instruction and formative assessment*. Council of Chief State School Officers, Washington, DC. Retrieved from www.ccsso.org/content/PDFs/FAST Learning Progressions.org

Heritage, M., Walqui, A., & Linquanti, R. (2015). *English language learners and the new standards: Developing language, content knowledge, and analytical practices in the classroom*. Cambridge, MA: Harvard Education Press.

National Research Council. (2007). *Taking science to school: Learning and teaching science in grades K–8*. Washington, DC: National Academies Press.

Panadero, E., & Jonsson, A. (2013). The use of scoring rubrics for formative assessment purposes revisited: A review. *Educational Research Review, 9*, 129–144. doi:10.1016/j.edurev.2013.01.002.

Panadero, E., & Romero, M. (2014). To rubric or not to rubric? The effects of self-assessment on self-regulation, performance and self-efficacy. *Assessment in Education: Principles, Policy & Practice, 21*(2), 133–148. doi:10.1080/0969594X.2013.877872

Perkins, D. (1992). *Smart schools: From training memories to educating minds*. New York, NY: The Free Press/Simon & Schuster.

Ross, J. A., & Starling, M. (2008). Self-assessment in a technology-supported environment: The case of grade 9 geography. *Assessment in Education: Principles, Policy and Practice, 15*(2), 183–199.

Sadler, D. R. (1989). Formative assessment and the design of instructional strategies. *Instructional Science, 18,* 119–144.

Seidel, T., Rimmele, R., & Prenzel, M. (2005). Clarity and coherence of lesson goals as a scaffold for student learning. *Learning and Instruction, 15*(6), 539–556.

Songer, N., Kelcey, B., & Gotwals, A. (2009). How and when does complex reasoning occur? Empirically driven development of a learning progression focused on complex reasoning about biodiversity. *Journal for Research in Science Teaching, 46*(6), 610–631.

Steedle, J. T., & Shavelson, R. J. (2009). Supporting valid interpretations of learning progression level diagnoses. *Journal of Research in Science Teaching, 46*(6), 699–715.

Sztajn, P., Confrey, J., Wilson, P. H., & Edgington, C. (2012). Learning trajectory based instruction: Toward a theory of teaching. *Educational Researcher, 41,* 147–156.

Wylie, C., Bauer, M., Bailey, A. L., & Heritage, M. (in press). Formative assessment of mathematics and language: What applying companion learning progressions can reveal to teachers. In A. L. Bailey, C. Mayer, & L. Wilkinson (Eds.), *Language, literacy and learning in the STEM disciplines: How language counts for English learners.* New York: Routledge.

Wylie, C., Ciofalo, J., & Mavronikolas, E. (2010). *Documenting, diagnosing and treating misconceptions: Impact on student learning.* Paper presentation at the annual meeting of the American Educational Research Association, Denver, CO.

4
Collecting and Interpreting Evidence of Learning

Overview

Chapter 4 is about how teachers can obtain evidence of learning so that they and their students can take responsive action to enhance the learning. We introduce classroom-tested methods for informally collecting and interpreting evidence as students work, as well as diagnostic items, parallel tests, and online assessment systems. Evidence quality in formative assessment is considered. Discussions of peer and self-assessment emphasize that students themselves can also be useful sources of evidence of learning, under the right conditions.

In Chapter 2 we stressed that formative classroom assessment is used by teachers and students to notice, recognize, and respond to student learning in order to enhance learning during the learning (e.g., Cowie & Bell, 1999; Swaffield, 2011). Once you have clear learning goals and closely aligned performance and/or product criteria, you determine when and how best to obtain evidence of learning during a lesson so that you, and your students, can take responsive action to enhance the learning. Just as criteria need to be aligned to the learning goals, sources of evidence need to be aligned to the criteria. For example, if a rubric has been designed to obtain evidence of the status of students' informational writing skills, it is obvious that a source of evidence will be the students' written work. Students can use the rubric to guide their writing and ultimately make determinations about the quality of their essay by assessing their own work with the rubric.

Similarly, if a performance criterion for the goal "understanding how the structure of DNA relates to its function" is "to explain why the base pair rule means DNA forms complementary strands and a double helix," then the teacher would need to elicit an explanation from the students during the course of learning about this phenomenon. While students are in the process of learning about the base pair rule, they will have in mind that they should be able to provide such an explanation, and can take action if they judge that they are having difficulty in formulating an explanation from their current understanding.

Teachers collect evidence of learning in myriad ways: via conversations with students, while watching and listening as they work, and by reviewing written performances. From the evidence obtained, teachers make a determination of the gap between the students' current status and the desired goal, often during the course of a lesson. For example, the evidence may reveal that some students have a fundamental misconception, while other students are close to meeting the goal.

Obtaining and interpreting evidence demands a high level of expertise on the part of a teacher, which has been referred to as teacher *connoisseurship* (Cowie, 2016). Undergirding *connoisseurship* are several competencies, including strong, flexible disciplinary knowledge, an understanding of which formative assessment strategies are most effective for the subject learning at hand, and knowledge of how student learning of that content develops.

Collecting and Interpreting Evidence as Students Work

We will illustrate *connoisseurship* with two middle school examples, both of which demonstrate Principle 1: Assessment is integrated into the process of teaching and learning. The first is a science example drawn from Stanford Educational Assessment Laboratory's curriculum unit *Why Things Sink and Float* (relative density) (Shavelson et al., 2008). After several related activities and discussions about why certain objects sink and others float, the teacher asks pairs of students to make a representation (their choice) about why they think things sink or float. While the students are working, she circulates round the classroom and notes that some students are representing the phenomenon in terms of mass or volume only, others are showing the mass/volume relationship and what it has to do with sinking and floating, and a few pairs are representing the mass/volume relationship and how objects sink or float based on what they are made of and the liquid in which they are floating (relative density). The teacher is making these judgments about students' learning status in real time, and asks questions to probe the students' thinking further to understand what responsive action she needs to take, either there and then or in the next lesson.

It is hard to imagine how the teacher could have interpreted evidence appropriately without the *connoisseurship* competencies described above—deep understandings of the discipline, formative assessment, and student learning. It is also worth noting that the process of identifying the building blocks of standards described in Chapter 3 helps teachers make real-time determinations of where students are in their learning.

The second example of connoisseurship is from a mathematics lesson on coordinate grids (Heritage, 2010). The teacher, Sharon Pernisi, had discussed the learning goals and performance criteria in Table 4.1 with her sixth-grade students.

While she was planning her lesson, Ms. Pernisi had also identified some challenges that the students might experience so that she could be alert for them.

- Students may have a procedural graphing misconception—(y, x)
- Plot points in spaces rather than intersections
- Count intervals on lines rather than x- or y-axes

Table 4.1 Ms. Pernisi's Learning Goals and Performance Criteria for Sixth-Grade Lesson on Coordinate Grids

Math Learning Goals	*Performance Criteria*
Understand the structure of a coordinate grid	1. I can talk and write about plotting points on a coordinate grid using correct vocabulary.
Relate the procedure of plotting points to the structure of a coordinate grid	2. I can plot and label points in each quadrant on a coordinate grid.
	3. I can create a rule about coordinates for each quadrant.

In the middle of the lesson, Ms. Pernisi asked students in their groups to label each location on a large piece of graph paper (aligned to criterion 2) and describe the process verbally using correct vocabulary (aligned to criterion 1). As she observed the students' activity, she noted that some students were plotting points in spaces rather than intersections, and their vocabulary use was minimal (in line with her identified challenges). Others were counting intervals on lines rather than on the x- or y-axes, and were using some appropriate vocabulary. A number of students could accurately identify and plot x and y coordinates and use appropriate vocabulary to explain the process of identification and plotting. Ms. Pernisi was able to make these real-time interpretations because of her careful planning before the lesson, and to respond to learning during the course of the lesson so that students could make progress with plotting points or, in the case of the latter group of students, move to creating rules for coordinates.

These two middle school examples show how teachers elicited and interpreted evidence in the ongoing flow of activity and interactions in the classroom (Swaffield, 2011), as student learning was unfolding: Principle 1 in action.

Other, more formal assessments are also effective for diagnosing students' problems, as well as accomplishments, because they are intentionally designed to reflect common gaps, errors, and misconceptions. For example, at the beginning of a new unit or topic, students can be given a set of statement cards (e.g., "multiplication always makes numbers bigger," "you cannot divide by 0," etc.) and asked to sort them into three piles: agree, disagree, don't know (Hodgen & Wiliam, 2006). Students sort the cards, preferably in pairs or small groups, thereby activating prior knowledge while also indicating to themselves and the teachers what topics and skills need the most attention.

This activity can be revisited at the end of the unit to assess what students learned. Carefully selected diagnostic items (see below and the example in Chapter 2) can also provide evidence of learning and guide teachers' interpretations.

Collecting and Interpreting Evidence of Learning From Diagnostic Items

Diagnostic items provide information not just about whether or not students know and can do something, but also about specific learning needs that can inform next steps. Chappuis (2015) points out that instructionally tractable assessments indicate whether students' performance reflects errors due to (1) incomplete understanding (they haven't been learning it wrong; they just haven't learned it yet), (2) flaws in reasoning (e.g., overgeneralizing when learning to generalize), (3) misconceptions, or (4) something else.

For an example of an item that diagnoses specific gaps in students' learning, see the second item in Figure 4.1 (Chappuis, 2015). In order to diagnose student learning, the distractors, or wrong answer choices, in the second selected response item are not simply wrong. Each distractor is wrong in a way that reflects a common gap or misconception.

The great benefit of diagnostic assessments is that the teacher can avoid re-teaching a whole lesson (an all-too-common practice), but can instead target instruction on what, specifically, tripped up the students. In this way, good assessment can "short-circuit the randomness and inefficiency of trial and error learning" (Sadler, 1989, p. 120).

There is some evidence that diagnostic, multiple-choice items are actually better than open-ended items at eliciting students' true understanding, perhaps because the items

> Consider the following item:
>
> Which fraction is largest?
> a) 1/3   b) 2/5   c) 7/9
>
> It is likely that many fourth-grade students would be able to correctly choose answer choice *c*, because both the numerator and the denominator are the largest numbers in the set given. This set of answer choices doesn't accurately differentiate between students who understand the concept and students who don't. Students could get it right for the right reason (understanding it is the relationship between the numerator and the denominator that determines size) or for the wrong reason (believing that size is determined by the numerator or by the denominator). The item also doesn't help ferret out misconceptions that may be lurking.
>
> On the other hand, consider the answer choices in this problem:
>
> Which fraction is largest?
>
> a) 2/1   b) 3/8   c) 4/3
>
> Students who understand that it is the relationship between the numerator and the denominator that determines size will likely choose answer *a*. Students who use the denominator to determine size will likely choose answer *b*. Students who use the numerator to determine size will likely choose answer *c*. With answer choices like these, you not only know who does and doesn't understand magnitude in fractions, you also know what to focus on with students who have selected each wrong answer choice.

Figure 4.1 Diagnostic Item on Fractions

Source: Chappuis (2015, p. 212)

probe students' thinking by offering plausible incorrect answers (Steedle & Shavelson, 2009). It's the word *plausible* that matters here: humorous or throwaway distractors are not instructionally tractable, but incorrect answers that demonstrate incomplete understanding, errors in reasoning, or misconceptions are useful to teachers, who can use them to identify next steps in instruction.

A freely available and very useful assessment designed to provide diagnostic information is the aptly named DIAGNOSER, an interactive Web-based program with a variety of assessment and instructional tools for middle and high school mathematics and science (www.diagnoser.com; Minstrell, Anderson, Kraus, & Minstrell, 2008). The tools can be integrated into teachers' existing curriculum units. The developers provide suggestions about which tools can be used in specific phases of teacher-designed units.

As in the fractions item in Figure 4.1, each item in DIAGNOSER reflects a different conception or misconception. A primer provides guidance for pencil-and-paper "elicitation" questions for use in the opening stages of the unit, with suggestions for how to promote student thinking, participation, and commitment to an answer through discussion. The purpose of this assessment is to provide the teacher with an initial idea of the students' thinking.

The next assessments are computer-based multiple-choice, numerical response, and short-answer items designed to target specific facets of student thinking. Students' responses give teachers diagnostic information, and DIAGNOSER provides sample lessons that address misconceptions. Students receive feedback as they work through their assignments, and teachers can view reports that detail their students' thinking about the assigned topic. See the section entitled Collecting and Interpreting Evidence of Learning With Technology, see page 76, for additional examples of computer-based programs that provide evidence of learning.

Other sources of diagnostic items for science teaching include Sadler (1998) for astronomy and space, Shavelson and his colleagues (2008) for buoyancy, and Ciofalo and Wylie (Ciofalo & Wylie, 2006; Wylie, Ciofalo, & Mavronikolas, 2010) for math and science. Teachers who write diagnostic assessments on their own might consider creating a template or formula for distractors (Chappuis, 2015). Chappuis (p. 214) offers the following example.

If a learning target is to understand how to make generalizations, a teacher could assign a short passage about meat-eating plants and then pose this open-ended question: What generalization can you make from this passage about how meat-eating plants lure their prey? Students' responses could be sorted into three or four categories:

a. Correct answer with a statement that is true for the evidence presented and generalizes logically to a broader array of instances
b. Partially correct answer that is true for the evidence presented but includes too broad an array of instances (overgeneralization)
c. True for the evidence presented but without an extension to other instances (no generalization)
d. Incorrect answer that is not true for the evidence presented and/or does not extend to other instances (incorrect interpretation)

Using the four categories as a template, the teacher can write answers to a question that are not just correct and incorrect but also reveal types of learning needs that indicate next teaching moves. The action a teacher takes depends on the results of the (hopefully formative) test. If the preponderance of student responses are a), the teacher can move on to a new learning goal. If there are a significant number of b) responses, she must teach about overgeneralization and how to avoid it. A lot of c) responses indicate that the concept of generalization must be taught again in a new way, and too many d) responses might prompt a check of students' understanding of the passage.

Collecting and Interpreting Evidence of Learning From Parallel Tests

Much as individual items can be used diagnostically, entire multiple-choice tests can deepen learning if they are used to identify and fill in gaps in students' knowledge and skills, rather than simply to generate a score for a grade file (which they can also do, of course). Instead of simply going over the answers on a summative test and moving on, you can involve students in analyzing tests to see which questions and concepts were causing the most problems (Hodgen & Wiliam, 2006). Of course, this analytical process is not useful unless it is followed by instruction that addresses the problems by teaching them in new ways, since the first way did not work for all students. An especially powerful, student-centered, formative use of summative tests is called parallel testing (Bloom, 1984). This idea has been around for a long time but is only recently getting the renewed attention it deserves. It is based on Benjamin Bloom's (1971) work on mastery learning.

In his research, Bloom compared conventional teaching to mastery learning. In the conventional classrooms, 30 students were given tests only for purposes of determining grades. In the mastery learning classrooms, 30 students had the same teacher and the same curriculum, but formative tests were given for the purposes of feedback. The formative tests were followed by corrective procedures that filled in gaps in students' understanding. Then the students took parallel (same content, but different questions) summative tests to determine their mastery of the subject matter.

The results of Bloom's experiments with mastery learning were quite impressive (Bloom, 1984). The average student under mastery learning did better than 84% of the students in the conventional class. Seventy percent of the mastery learning students attained the level of summative achievement reached by only the highest 20% of the students in the conventional class. In addition, mastery learning students spent 75% of their time on task, compared to 65% under conventional instruction. All students, including the low and high achievers, tended to do better in mastery classrooms than students in the conventional classes, who were given summative tests once at the end of a unit, without benefit of the feedback provided by a formative test and the gap-filling learning activities before the summative test.

It is important to note that Bloom did not just give "practice tests," a common technique for which there is little evidence of effectiveness. Simply having students take a practice test and then going over the answers puts students in a relatively passive role because it is the teacher that reveals the answers. A better approach requires students to actively *think* about what they do and do not know, and takes only a few more minutes.

One of us (Heidi) became so enamored with this idea that she added a parallel quiz to a class that had been test-free until that time. In order to both build and demonstrate understanding of formatting references and citations using the style guidelines of the American Psychological Association (APA style), Heidi now teaches the rules of formatting, then gives a formative quiz. Before going over the quiz, she has pairs of students compare their answers. When they disagree on an answer, they use their resources, including the Internet, to figure out which one is right, thereby filling in gaps in their knowledge. Then they repeat the process with another pair, until they believe they have all the right answers and, most importantly, understand why they are right. Only then does Heidi go over the correct answers with the whole class, just to be sure everyone has them.

(They always do, but she cannot resist.) When the class meets again, the students take the summative quiz that counts for a grade.

The results in Heidi's classroom echo Bloom's research: Everyone gets a higher score on the summative quiz than on the formative one unless, of course, they were 100% correct the first time. The higher achievement is arguably due to the fact that students had to think together about what they did not know after they took the formative test. Bloom (1984) would agree: "The main point is that the mastery learning students [those who received corrective feedback on tests] improve their processing of the instruction, although the instruction is much the same in both types of classes" (p. 8). Because *learning is a consequence of thinking* (Perkins, 1992), the effects of parallel testing on achievement are predictable: Students learn more when they identify gaps in their knowledge and think about how to fill them in than when the teacher does all the thinking for them.

Collecting and Interpreting Evidence of Learning With Technology

Assessment technologies are designed to give feedback to students about their progress, and to enable teachers to respond to the learning needs of each student with greater speed, frequency, focus, and flexibility. The features of student-centered assessment technologies include: (1) systematic monitoring of student progress to inform instructional decisions; (2) identification of misconceptions that may interfere with student learning; (3) rapid feedback to students, teachers, and others; and (4) information about student learning needs during instruction (Russell,

2010). Computer-based assessment programs integrate the management of learning (organizing student assignments and assessments), curricular resources, embedded assessments, and detailed student-level and class-level reports. Perhaps the greatest advantage of computerized systems is the degree to which they help students and teachers monitor progress by responding to each student's work in detail and with immediacy. There is currently no shortage of technological tools that are intended to support teachers' classroom formative assessment, including those created by researchers and online response systems for which teachers either create or select the assessment items. First, we describe some researcher-developed tools.

Researcher-Developed Tools

FACT is a distributed system for in-class use that facilitates the use of Classroom Challenges (CCs) developed by the Mathematics Assessment Project (http://map.mathshell.org/). The CCs promote specific classroom practices, including collaborative learning, discussion, and reflection, with emphasis on rich problem-solving tasks and formative feedback. In their original format, the CCs are entirely paper-based. FACT lets students work on Android tablets equipped with styli and enables a teacher to manage the class and to orchestrate the activities required by the CCs. The student interface helps teachers by analyzing student work, making suggestions about what to say to students, and identifying points for intervention. As the authors of FACT note, "FACT aims to be an unobtrusive helper in the classroom" (Cheema, Pead, VanLehn, Schoenfeld, & Burkhardt, 2016, p. 5).

ASSISTments, developed at Worcester Polytechnic Institute, makes use of digital teaching platforms to blend assessment and assistance in a tool that can be adapted and used in a variety of ways, primarily with mathematics content. ASSISTments offers teachers in grades 3 to high school pre-built content that includes assessment items and tutoring opportunities aligned to the Common Core State Standards for Mathematics (CCSSM). Both the items and the tutoring content are editable, so if the items are not completely aligned to the teacher's learning goals and performance criteria derived from the CCSSM, the teacher can modify them. Additionally, teachers can write their own items that correspond more closely to the goals of the immediate learning. Item types include short answer, open-response, multiple choice, and check all that apply. Questions can also be embedded into content videos. During the lesson, students can respond to questions and anonymously post the answers using a projector or interactive whiteboard.

SimScientists are simulation-based science assessments developed by WestEd, with funding from the National Science Foundation, and intended to assess students' knowledge of earth, life, and physical science concepts. Benchmark assessments are designed to test end-of-unit achievement, whereas a set of shorter assessments is designed for use during the unit. According to the assessment designers, these shorter assessments function as formative resources in three ways: (1) by providing immediate feedback contingent on an individual student's performance, (2) by offering graduated levels of coaching in real time, and (3) by providing diagnostic information to guide offline reflection and extension activities (Quellmalz, Timms, & Buckley, 2009). Teachers can create reports in the system to analyze individual and group progress. Obviously, SimScientists would only be used when the assessments clearly align with the learning goals that a teacher and students are pursuing.

Online Assessment Response Tools

The following vignette, excerpted from a March 2014 *Education Week* article, illustrates how various online assessment response tools can support teachers to obtain information about students' learning status.

> ### Text Box 4.1 Geometry Online Assessment Response Tool
>
> During a lesson in Brandon Thompson's geometry class, students used four separate classroom apps to learn about finding the area of triangles that contain no 90-degree angles. Despite the variety of tools being used in the classroom, the lesson went off without a hitch, with both teacher and students switching seamlessly among tools even though they had only been introduced a few months earlier.
>
> First, Mr. Thompson had the class download problems from *iTunes U*, a course-management tool from Apple Inc., and begin solving them in *Notability*, a digital note-taking app.
>
> Shortly after the students began, Mr. Thompson asked them to use the Socrative app to submit their solutions directly from their iPads to his. As he walked around the room, Mr. Thompson scrolled through a single screen that contained each student's name and response. One student appeared way off base; the teacher stopped by to work with him directly. Overall, the snapshot revealed that most students got the overall gist, although many made rounding mistakes and failed to properly notate the unit of analysis.
>
> Based on the information from Socrative and conversations with students as he circulated the room, Mr. Thompson then identified two—one of whose work illustrated the

> common misunderstandings and another whose work demonstrated a creative problem-solving approach—and asked them to "beam in." Using an app called *AirPlay*, the students projected the screens of their iPads onto a wall at the front of the room
>
> "Camille, would you talk us through what's going on here?" Mr. Thompson asked. A quick class-wide discussion served to both illuminate the process by which the student solved the problem and highlight the error made by much of the class. Murmurs of understanding rippled through the room. Mr. Thompson concluded that the class was ready to move on, so he repeated the process, but with a more difficult challenge: This time, students were asked to develop an original formula that would allow them to solve for the area of any non-right triangle.

One advantage of the technology is the display of students' problem-solving efforts on a single screen. This display enables Mr. Thompson to monitor responses and intervene immediately with one student. Notably, he also augmented the evidence on the screen with conversations as he circulated round the classroom, observing students' responses. Mr. Thompson was able to quickly see the mistakes the students made and take pedagogical action, selecting two students' solutions for the class to consider. These were quickly made available to the class through AirPlay. Importantly, he used these solutions to promote discussion and highlight errors, leading him to a decision that the students were ready to move on to a more challenging problem.

There are a number of other online response tools available to teachers, ranging from ones in which teachers create items, including multiple-choice, true/false, or short-answer questions, to one teachers can use to create multimedia presentations, or select published ones, and embed multiple-choice quizzes, slide shows, polls, draw-its (students write directly on a slide), and open-ended questions. In line with the adage "garbage in, garbage out," the quality of the items will dictate the quality of the feedback teachers get about learning, so teachers will need to create or select items that are clearly aligned to the learning goals and success criteria and that will provide them with instructionally tractable information.

In considering the affordances of online response tools in higher education, Beatty and Gerace (2009) note that they simultaneously provide anonymity and accountability. Students are held accountable for answering questions, and are provided anonymity because the individual answers to questions and prompts do not need to be revealed—an aggregate class view can show how many students picked each answer, correct or incorrect. The fact that students may need accountability and desire anonymity may say more about the nature of the classroom culture than the benefits of the response system.

Beatty and Gerace (2009) also observe that online response tools support collecting answers from all students in a class, rather than just the few who routinely speak up or are called upon to respond. Of course, a no-hands-up policy with techniques for randomly calling on students can obviate this issue. Taking a cue from Mr. Thompson, the more that teachers can discuss with students the reason for their responses, the richer the information they will have to act on.

Evidence Quality

Thus far in this chapter we have discussed a wide variety of assessments that teachers can use to collect and interpret evidence of student learning. Students themselves can also be useful sources of such evidence—we will explain why and how in a few pages. But first, it seems important to address the matter of the *quality* of the assessments that teachers design and use. After all, low-quality assessments are likely to provide misinformation about student learning, which can lead to ineffective action on the part of the teacher. This, of course, is something the use of formative assessment is intended to avoid. So, in this section, we discuss important concepts related to assessment quality from traditional psychometric perspectives (i.e., methods for construction of measurement instruments and procedures for measurement) and then consider these concepts in the context of formative assessment.

Validity is the central concept that defines assessment quality; it is the extent to which an assessment provides accurate information for making decisions about student learning, and the adequacy and appropriateness of the use of assessment results for specific purposes. While people often refer to the "validity of an assessment," it is more correct to refer to the degree to which evidence and theory support the *interpretations* that can be made from the results of an assessment (American Educational Research Association, American Psychological Association, National Council on Measurement in Education, Joint Committee on Standards for Educational & Psychological Testing [AERA, APA, NCME] 2014). Interpretations of results should not be thought of as valid or invalid. Rather, validity is a matter of degree based on evidence (Messick, 1995).

Construct validity is the overarching term to evaluate the validity of an assessment and involves collecting multiple types of validity evidence during all phases of assessment development and using the evidence to justify that the assessment measures what it claims to measure. An example of an assessment that lacks construct validity is a new fourth-grade math test with tenth-grade vocabulary in the word problems. That test cannot be said to test students' math skills because the sophisticated vocabulary is likely to prevent them from doing the problems, whether they know the math or not. Evidence of construct validity—for example, testing students' math skills in a different way and comparing the results to the new math tests—determines the degree to which an assessment's content is relevant to, and representative of, the construct being assessed.

Fairness is another fundamental validity issue that requires attention through all stages of assessment development and use (AERA, APA, NCME, 2014). Assessment developers and users need to be able to answer the question, "How can we best enable all students to show what they know and can do?" Ensuring that assessments measure the intended construct and minimizing the potential for construct irrelevance such as linguistic or cultural factors are the responsibility of assessment developers and users, including teachers (Doğan, 2016).

Reliability is a necessary component of validity and refers to how consistently an assessment measures what it is intended to measure. If an assessment is reliable, the results should be replicable. For instance, a change in the time of administration, day and time of scoring, who scores the assessment, and in the sample of assessment items should not create inconsistencies in results. That is, a child who has not received additional instruction between the administration of two very similar tests should get about the same score, even if different people rate it. If assessment results are not consistent, then it is reasonable to conclude that the scores do not accurately measure what the assessment is intended to measure.

Reliability estimates indicate the degree to which scores are free from measurement error. Each type of reliability estimate should have a reliability coefficient, represented by the letter "r" and expressed as a number ranging between 0.00 and 1.00. Reliability coefficients of 0.8 and up are typically regarded as moderate to high, while coefficients below 0.6 are low.

Professional psychometricians establish validity, fairness, and reliability for many educational measures such as the end-of-year state assessments, whereas formative assessment relies on the clinical judgment of teachers about students' responses day by day in the classroom (Erickson, 2007). Nonetheless, issues of validity, fairness, and reliability are important considerations in the practice of formative assessment.

Validity in Formative Assessment

The concept of validity can and should be applied to formative assessment. The evidence generated by the variety of means discussed in this chapter is intended to provide information about the students' learning status in relation to the specific learning goals, and to be used to inform decisions about next steps in teaching and learning. In formative assessment, the construct being assessed is the lesson-learning goal, so alignment between the assessment method and the goal is an important validity concern. Teachers will need to ask: "Is this assessment method going to provide me with information related to this specific learning goal?"

In addition, the assessment method the teacher selects should be an appropriate representation of the construct, and include the important dimensions of the construct. In other words, the way a teacher decides to obtain evidence should not be so broad that it contains dimensions that are irrelevant to the construct, nor so narrow that it fails to include the important dimensions of the construct. For example, if the learning goal is for students to apply their knowledge about the nature of gradation to their drawings, then a method to gather evidence of this application that includes neatness and the proper use of art materials, in addition to the nature of gradation, represents construct irrelevance. Similarly, an assessment method to obtain evidence of students' learning status with respect to asking and answering questions about text that focuses only on answering questions is not fully relevant to the construct.

A further validity concern in formative assessment is consequential validity (Stobart, 2006). Action resulting from the use of formative assessment evidence is intended to result in benefits to student learning. Therefore, if advances in learning do not result from the use of formative assessment evidence, then the issue of validity should be addressed in terms of an investigation of why the assessment and its use were not successful (Stobart, 2008). In the same vein, Crooks, Kane, and Cohen (1996) identified "pedagogical decisions" as an important factor in the validity of formative assessment, noting that two students who had performed similarly on a task might benefit from differential pedagogical responses and encouragement based on their personal preferences and needs.

Reliability in Formative Assessment

Reliability is less critical for classroom assessment because errors in instructional decisions can be quickly rectified by gathering more evidence of learning (Shepard, 2001). Even so, it is important for teachers to be aware of reliability in the context of formative assessment. In a useful formulation, psychometrician Jeffrey Smith refers to reliability in relation to instructional decisions as "sufficiency of information" (2003, p. 30). What this means is that teachers have to be confident that they have *enough* information about a student's learning to make a decision about pedagogical action. For example, a teacher might observe a student making an error while solving a mathematical problem, but would be in a better position to make a decision about what to do if she had asked the student to explain his thinking and the reasons for solving the problem in that particular way.

Fairness in Formative Assessment

In the same way that fairness is applicable in traditional psychometric approaches, it is also relevant to formative assessment. Because students do not learn in lockstep, formative assessment is inevitably personalized and teachers will need to employ methods that tap into the individual student's learning status. An important concern regarding fairness, and indeed equity, is that whatever methods teachers select, they should account for the range of students present in the class so that all students have the opportunity to show where they are in their learning and have the prospect of moving forward from their current status. Similarly, formative assessment methods should not include any elements that would prevent some students from showing where they are relative to goals, such as the use of language they cannot understand.

Using the Evidence

Teachers' use of evidence is dealt with in the next chapter, so here we note just a few points that are relevant to obtaining and using evidence. First, assessment information needs to be interpreted so that teachers can make a determination of students' current learning status. This is another instance where learning progressions can be useful by providing the framework for interpretation. Second, even before the evidence is generated, teachers will need to have the knowledge and skills to formulate or select evidence-gathering methods that reveal the nature of student understanding or skills. Third, evidence gathering is a planned process with assessment methods having a "place in the 'rhythm' of the instruction, built-in as part of the constant interaction that is essential to ensure that the teacher and the learner are mutually and closely involved to a common purpose" (Black, Wilson, & Yao, 2011, p. 98).

Ensuring assessment has a place in the rhythm of instruction means that teachers will need to plan in advance when and from whom they will need evidence of learning. Of course, this does not preclude actionable assessment opportunities arising spontaneously in the lesson, but rather that evidence gathering should not be left to chance (Heritage, 2013). In the next section, we turn to students' collecting and using their own assessment information.

Collecting and Interpreting Evidence of Learning From Themselves: Student Self-Assessment

Teachers are not the sole source of judgment of student learning in the classroom. Under the right conditions, students themselves can analyze learning and recommend next steps via peer and self-assessment. When we first investigated self- and peer assessment, many teachers told us what they knew from their experience to be true: Peer and self-assessment are worthless because students would just give themselves As, stroke their friends, bash their enemies, and not revise their work. That is all more or less true, *if* you ask students to give themselves and each other grades that will count. That is a summative type of self- and peer assessment, and students are savvy: Knowing how the grading system works, many of them will give themselves good grades, quickly assign a grade to their peers, and assume they are done because grading only happens at the end.

However, self-assessment is not the same as self-evaluation, which is when students assign their own grades. The problems with self-grading are self-evident. If, on the other hand, we think of self-assessment as a formative process during which students reflect on the quality of their learning, judge the degree to which it reflects explicitly stated goals or criteria, and revise accordingly (Andrade, 2010), we see very different behaviors (at least after they get used to it). We see students taking control of their learning by finding the gaps between their current learning and the goals, and then using their own feedback to close the gaps. By engaging in self-assessment in this way, students are self-regulating their learning.

In order to make that happen, you need to support students in the three key steps of formative self-assessment: (1) understanding learning goals and criteria, (2) critiquing their learning in terms of those goals and criteria, and (3) revision of their ideas and/or work. Step three is crucial: Students must have opportunities to update their understandings of concepts and skills, and revise and improve their performances (Andrade, 2010).

Self-assessment has been investigated in many contexts, including elementary and middle school writing, middle school mathematics, and high school social studies and technology. For example, Heidi and her colleagues (Andrade, Du, & Mycek, 2010; Andrade, Du, & Wang,

2008) had third- through seventh-graders read a model essay or story and generate a list of criteria as a class. Using rubrics based on those criteria, as well as a highly scaffolded process that had them look for evidence of having met those criteria by underlining using colored pencils (Figure 4.2), students self-assessed drafts of their writing and revised according to their own feedback. That process is described and demonstrated in the self-assessment video found here: www.studentsatthecenter.org/resources/student-centered-assessment-video-suite.

Not surprisingly, the group that used the rubrics for self-assessment wrote better stories and essays than a comparison group that simply reviewed their work without the rubric or the scaffolded process. Ross, Hogaboam-Gray, and Rolheiser (2002) did something similar with fifth- and sixth-grade mathematics students, with comparable results. Their self-assessment instruction involved students in defining criteria, taught them how to apply the criteria, gave students feedback on their self-assessments, and helped them develop action plans based on those self-assessments. Again, the students who self-assessed using criteria outscored a comparison group at solving mathematics problems, probably because the self-assessment process engages students in thinking about the qualities of an effective solution, and then, armed with that understanding, taking a constructively critical look at their own work.

Self-assessment can also help teachers provide specific, targeted suggestions to students. Tina Montalvo, a fifth-grade theater arts teacher in Staten Island, New York, has her students use a co-created checklist to regularly reflect on which performance criteria they have met, and on which they need to work. Once students have identified something in need of attention, she can make specific suggestions for how to grow as actors. For example, one

	4	3	2	1
The claim	I make a claim and explain why it is controversial.	I make a claim but don't explain why it is controversial.	My claim is buried, confused and/or unclear.	I don't say what my argument or claim is.
Reasons in support of the claim	I give clear and accurate reasons in support of my claim.	I give reasons in support of my claim but I overlook important reasons.	I give 1 or 2 weak reasons that don't support my claim, and/or irrelevant or confusing reasons.	I do not give reasons in support of my claim.
Reasons against the claim	I discuss the reasons against my claim and explain why it is valid anyway.	I discuss the reasons against my claim but neglect some or don't explain why the claim still stands.	I say that there are reasons against the claim but I don't discuss them.	I do not acknowledge or discuss the reasons against the claim.
Organization	My writing has a compelling opening, an informative middle and a satisfying conclusion.	My writing has a beginning, middle and end.	My organization is rough but workable. I may sometimes get off topic.	My writing is aimless and disorganized.
Etc.				

Figure 4.2 Scaffolded Self-Assessment of a Persuasive Essay Draft (excerpt)

student noted that he needed to "use stillness" and "don't rush" when acting in the production of *Willy Wonka*. Ms. Montalvo was then able to provide individualized guidance by putting just one sentence on a Post-it Note: "When working on stillness, remember to stay focused and listening, or your mind will wander." Because the student had already identified the problem as one in need of a solution, her quickly generated recommendation was well received.

Self-assessment can play a significant role in self-regulated learning (Principle 3 again) when students use their self-assessments to monitor progress and plan next steps. Meusen-Beekman, Joosten-ten Brinke, and Boshuizen (2014) studied nearly 700 sixth-grade students in the Netherlands. Students in the treatment condition, which lasted 27 weeks, engaged in peer or self-assessment of three writing assignments. They also co-created the criteria for their writing, set goals, made plans, and used checklists to monitor their progress. Students in the treatment group were more self-regulated and had higher intrinsic motivation, with no differences between the peer and self-assessment conditions.

The research on student self-assessment is pretty clear: When students have opportunities to review and revise their own learning in light of the criteria for it, their performance improves. There is also reason to believe that self-assessment can promote self-regulated learning. This is one reason we are able to make that bold claim we made at the beginning of Chapter 1 about the effects of formative assessment on learning and achievement.

Collecting and Interpreting Evidence of Learning From Peers

Students' peers can also be a useful and readily available source of feedback. Several studies conducted in high

Figure 4.3 One Big Happy, Reprinted with Permission, Rick Detorie and Creators Syndicate, Inc.

schools have indicated that there is a relationship between peer assessment and achievement (Topping, 2013), and that peer feedback is helpful to both the assessed and the assessors. The caveat, of course, is that peer feedback must be carefully scaffolded in order to ensure it is constructive, rather than a matter of stroking one's friends and bashing one's enemies. Nearly everyone we ask has experienced really bad peer assessment like that seen in Figure 4.3.

How to avoid useless or demeaning peer assessment? It is essential that feedback focuses on the learning, rather than the individual, and that it includes specific suggestions for how to move the learning ahead. Students can give each other feedback using the same procedure outlined above for self-assessment (articulate goals and criteria, feedback, revision), but an additional element is also needed: Students must deliver feedback using a constructive process of critique. Some teachers of very young children like the Two Stars and a Wish approach (Figure 4.4), which is relatively self-explanatory.

An especially comprehensive and constructive critique protocol is called the Ladder of Feedback (Figure 4.5; Perkins, 2003). This protocol has four steps. The deliverer of the feedback: (1) asks questions of clarification about the

Interpreting Evidence of Learning 93

Figure 4.4 The Two Stars and a Wish Protocol for Constructive Peer Feedback

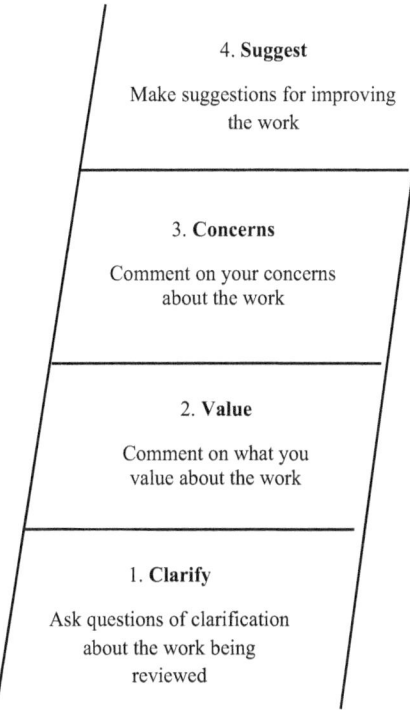

Figure 4.5 Ladder of Feedback

Source: Perkins (2003)

other student's work, (2) identifies aspects of the work that he or she values, (3) raises concerns about the work, and (4) offers suggestions for ways in which the work could be improved. See the peer assessment video here for a demonstration of the Ladder of Feedback in a middle school classroom: www.studentsatthecenter.org/resources/student-centered-assessment-video-suite.

Each step on the ladder is important (Perkins, 2003). The first step, asking questions of clarification, is often overlooked but should not be neglected because no one can give useful feedback on a piece of work that she or he does not understand. Ideas in the work may not be entirely clear, or some information might be missing. Clarifying by asking questions about unclear points or absent ideas helps students gather relevant information before informed feedback can be given.

The second step on the ladder, commenting on what is valued, involves expressing appreciation for aspects of the work. This step is fundamental to the process of constructive feedback. Valuing builds a supportive culture of understanding, and helps students identify strengths in their work they might not have recognized otherwise. Stressing the positive points of the work, noting strengths, and offering honest compliments set a supportive tone during a feedback session.

According to Perkins (2003), the third step is the time to raise concerns—not as derisive accusations or abrasive criticisms, but rather as honest thoughts and concerns. "Have you considered . . .?", "What I wonder about is . . .", "Perhaps you have thought about this, but . . ." are all ways of framing concerns in non-threatening ways. This step can be combined with the fourth. Giving suggestions for solving the problems identified during the Concerns step can help a learner use the feedback to make improvements and deepen learning. There is no guarantee that the learner will use the suggestions, nor need there be one. Suggestions are just that—suggestions—not mandates. The student receiving feedback maintains control over decisions about revisions and next steps.

Protocols like the Ladder of Feedback help teachers create constructive cultures of critique in their classrooms. If your classrooms are like ours, it will take time and effort to teach students how to faithfully use a protocol, but the results will be palpable: Within days, students will be talking to each other about what they are working on, and using each other's ideas to move their own ahead. When a protocol like the ladder is combined with criteria by using a checklist or rubric to ground peer feedback, you will also notice that students will use the vocabulary of your discipline in new, sophisticated ways.

Implementing peer assessment takes not only time and effort, at least at first, but also requires you to trust in students' ability to behave well when the right conditions are in place. Rules such as "We only give positive feedback" are sometimes implemented in classrooms where peer assessment has been attempted without criteria and/or a protocol. When, in contrast, students know what counts and use a thoughtful feedback process, they can and will raise substantive concerns and provide useful, often highly insightful suggestions for revision.

Student Interpretations of Feedback

Regardless of the source of feedback—teachers, peers, technologies, or students themselves—the action taken by a learner in response to the feedback depends, in part, on the way in which it was received (Black & Wiliam, 1998). Receiving feedback involves interpreting it, which is step I in Figure 1.2 in Chapter 1. Studies of the effects of students' interpretations of feedback on learning and achievement are scarce, but well-reasoned theories can focus our attention on the influential process of interpreting feedback.

Draper (2009) stresses how students' interpretations of ambiguous feedback determine whether that feedback is useful or not. He imagines that students can interpret feedback in six possible ways:

1. Technical knowledge or method, e.g., concluding that you did not use the best information or method for the task, both of which can be improved.
2. Effort, e.g., deciding that you did not leave enough time to do a task well.
3. Method of learning about a task, e.g., realizing that you did not seek out the right information, or did not understand the criteria for the task.
4. Ability, e.g., believing that you do not have the necessary aptitude to succeed at a task.
5. Random, e.g., assuming nothing was done incorrectly so success is possible next time without adjustment or revision.
6. The judgment process was wrong, e.g., determining that the feedback was incorrect.

Students' responses to feedback are likely to be determined by which of the above six interpretations are brought to bear on any given instance of feedback. Assuming that interpretations 1, 2, and 3 are generally (though not always) more productive than 4, 5, and 6, Draper urges teachers to help students construct appropriate interpretations of feedback by offering clear, often very simple, cues. The cues should indicate which interpretation of feedback is correct and constructive, for example, "This is a simple technical issue: You did not use the correct formula to use to solve this problem" (1: Technical method), or "Have you spent enough time and effort on this to do a good job?" (2: Effort), or "It might be helpful to review your method of learning about this task. How did you interpret the third criterion on the rubric?" (3: Method of learning).

The purpose of collecting and interpreting evidence from the teacher, technology, and students themselves is to act on the evidence, to move learning on. In the next chapter, we focus on the actions that teachers and students can take in response to evidence in order to keep learning moving forward.

References

American Educational Research Association, American Psychological Association, National Council on Measurement in Education, Joint Committee on Standards for Educational & Psychological Testing (US). (2014). *Standards for educational and psychological testing*. Washington, DC: American Educational Research Association.

Andrade, H. L. (2010). Students as the definitive source of formative assessment. In H. Andrade & G. Cizek (Eds.), *Handbook of formative assessment* (pp. 90–105). New York, NY: Routledge.

Andrade, H., Du, Y., & Mycek, K. (2010). Rubric-referenced self-assessment and middle school students' writing. *Assessment in Education*, *17*(2), 199–214.

Andrade, H., Du, Y., & Wang, X. (2008). Putting rubrics to the test: The effect of a model, criteria generation, and rubric-referenced self-assessment on elementary school students' writing. *Educational Measurement: Issues and Practices*, *27*(2), 3–13.

Beatty, I. D., & Gerace, W. J. (2009) Technology-enhanced formative assessment: A research-based pedagogy for teaching science with classroom response technology. *Journal of Science Education and Technology*. Retrieved from http://link.springer.com/article/10.1007/s10956-008-9140-4/fulltext.html

Black, P., & Wiliam, D. (1998). Assessment and classroom learning. *Assessment in Education: Principles Policy and Practice*, *5*, 7–73.

Black, P., Wilson, M., & Yao, S.-Y. (2011). Road maps for learning: A guide to the navigation of learning progressions. *Measurement: Interdisciplinary Research and Perspectives*, 9(2–3), 71–122.

Bloom, B. S. (1971). Mastery learning. In J. H. Block (Ed.), *Mastery learning: Theory and practice* (pp. 47–63). New York, NY: Holt, Rinehart and Winston.

Bloom, B. S. (1984). The search for methods of group instruction as effective as one-to-one tutoring. *Educational Leadership*, 41(8), 4–17.

Chappuis, J. (2015). *Seven strategies of assessment for learning* (2nd ed.). Upper Saddle River, NJ: Pearson Education.

Cheema, S., Pead, D., VanLehn, K., Schoenfeld, A., & Burkhardt, H. (2016). *Electronic posters to support formative assessment*. Proceeding of the 2016 CHI Conference Extended Abstracts in Computing Systems (pp. 1159–1164). Retrieved from http://dx.doi.org/10.1145/2851581.2892417

Ciofalo, J. F., & Wylie, E. C. (2006). Using diagnostic classroom assessment: One question at a time. *TCRecord*. Retrieved from www.tcrecord.org. ID Number: 12285.

Cowie, B. (April 2016). *Connoisseurship in formative assessment*. Presentation at the FAST SCASS Conference, Portland, OR.

Cowie, B., & Bell, B. (1999). A model of formative assessment in science education. *Assessment in Education: Principles, Policy & Practice*, 6(1), 101–116.

Crooks, T., Kane, M., & Cohen, A. (1996). Threats to the valid use of assessments. *Assessment in Education*, 3, 265–285.

Doğan, E. (2016). *The future is here: The (new) standards for educational and psychological testing*. National Council of Education Statistics. Retrieved from www.niss.org/sites/default/files/news_attachments/New%20standards%20Jan%2012%202015%20final_0.pdf

Draper, S. (2009). What are learners actually regulating when given feedback? *British Journal of Educational Technology*, 40(2), 306–315.

Education Week. (2014). *Testing digital tools to improve formative assessments*. Retrieved from www.edweek.org/ew/articles/2014/03/13/25personalized.h33.html?intc=EW-TC14-TOC

Erickson, F. (2007). Some thoughts on "proximal" formative assessment of student learning. *Yearbook of the National Society for the Study of Education*, 106, 186–216.

Heritage, M. (2010). *Formative assessment: Making it happen in the classroom.* Thousand Oaks, CA: Corwin Press.

Heritage, M. (2013). *Formative assessment: A process of inquiry and action.* Cambridge, MA: Harvard Education Press.

Hodgen, J., & Wiliam, D. (2006). *Mathematics inside the box: Assessment for learning in the mathematics classroom.* West Palm Beach, FL: Learning Sciences International.

Messick, S. (1995). Validity of psychological assessment. *American Psychologist, 50,* 741–749.

Meusen-Beekman, K., Joosten-ten Brinke, D., & Boshuizen, H. (2014). *The effects of formative assessment on self-regulated learning skills by sixth grade pupils.* Paper presented at the Conference of EARLI SIG1: Assessment and Evaluation, Madrid, Spain.

Minstrell, J., Anderson, R., Kraus, P., & Minstrell, J. E. (2008). Bridging from practice to research and back: Perspectives and tools in assessing for learning. In J. Coffey, R. Douglas, & C. Stearns (Eds.), *Assessing science learning* (pp. 37–69). Arlington, VA: National Science Teachers Association.

Perkins, D. (1992). *Smart schools: From training memories to educating minds.* New York, NY: The Free Press/Simon & Schuster.

Perkins, D. (2003). *King Arthur's round table: How collaborative conversations create smart organizations* (pp. 39–61). Hoboken, NJ: John Wiley & Sons.

Quellmalz, E. S., Timms, M., & Buckley, B. (2009). *Using science simulations to support powerful formative assessments of complex science learning.* Paper presented at the annual meeting of the American Educational Research Association, San Diego, CA.

Ross, J. A., Hogaboam-Gray, A., & Rolheiser, C. (2002). Student self-evaluation in grade 5–6 mathematics: Effects on problem-solving achievement. *Educational Assessment, 8,* 43–58.

Russell, M. (2010). Technology-aided formative assessment of learning. In H. Andrade & G. Cizek (Eds.), *Handbook of formative assessment* (pp. 125–138). New York: Routledge.

Sadler, D. R. (1989). Formative assessment and the design of instructional strategies. *Instructional Science, 18,* 119–144.

Sadler, P. (1998). Psychometric models of student conceptions in science: Reconciling qualitative studies and distractor-driven assessment instruments. *Journal of Research in Science Teaching, 35,* 265–296.

Shavelson, R., Young, D., Ayala, C., Brandon, P., Furtak, E., & Ruiz-Primo, M. (2008). On the impact of curriculum-embedded formative assessment on learning: A collaboration between curriculum and assessment developers. *Applied Measurement in Education*, 21, 295–314.

Shepard, L. A. (2001). The role of classroom assessment in teaching and learning. In V. Richardson (Ed.), *Handbook of research on teaching* (4th ed., pp. 1066–1101). Washington, DC: AERA.

Smith, J. (2003). Reconsidering reliability in classroom assessment and grading. *Educational Measurement: Issues and Practice*, 22(4), 26–33.

Steedle, J., & Shavelson, R. (2009). Supporting valid interpretations of learning progression level diagnoses. *Journal of Research in Science Teaching*, 46(6), 699–715.

Stobart, G. (2006). The validity of formative assessment. In J. Gardner (Ed.), *Assessment and Learning* (pp. 133–146). London: Sage.

Stobart, G. (November 2008). *Validity in formative assessment*. Paper presented at the Ninth Annual AEA-Europe Conference, Hisar, Bulgaria.

Swaffield, S. (2011). Getting to the heart of authentic assessment for learning. *Assessment in Education: Principles, Policy and Practice*, 18(4), 433–449.

Topping, K. J. (2013). Peers as a source of formative and summative assessment. In J. H. McMillan (Ed.), *SAGE handbook of research on classroom assessment* (pp. 395–412). London: Sage.

Wylie, C., Ciofalo, J., & Mavronikolas, E. (2010). *Documenting, diagnosing and treating misconceptions: Impact on student learning*. Paper presentation at the annual meeting of the American Educational Research Association, Denver, CO.

5
Taking Action

Overview

This chapter is based on the supposition that if no action is taken in response to the evidence obtained about learning, then it is not formative assessment. The first part of the chapter addresses the actions teachers can take based on evidence of learning, with suggestions for how to take immediate action and plan subsequent lessons. The second part of the chapter addresses student action. This section introduces the assessment strategies used by several teachers that prompt students to make corrections, rethink their ideas, and make revisions connected to learning goals and success criteria.

As we have discussed in earlier chapters, the focus of classroom formative assessment is to inform learning rather than measuring or summing it up. Teachers and students obtain evidence of learning during the course of a lesson so that they can take contingent action to keep learning moving forward.

Teachers Taking Action

In Chapter 4 we discussed teachers' interpretation of the evidence they intentionally gather to keep track of how student learning is progressing. Once you have interpreted the evidence, often in real time, you have to decide what you are going to do in response. Basically, you have three courses of action: (1) continue with the lesson as planned; (2) make immediate instructional adjustments; and (3) make plans for subsequent lessons. In each case, you are making pedagogical decisions that are founded on evidence of students' current learning status.

Continue With the Lesson as Planned

It may be that you decide to obtain evidence of student learning at a strategic point in a lesson to ensure that students understand the basis of an idea before they move to the next part of the lesson that extends the idea. For example, in Chapter 4 we saw that Sharon Pernisi, a sixth-grade teacher, intentionally captured evidence of student understanding of plotting points on a coordinate grid. If, instead of finding that her students had some misunderstandings of this idea, she had discovered that students were solid in their understanding, Ms. Pernisi would have made a decision to carry on with the next phase of the lesson, which involved plotting points in each quadrant. Similarly, in an eighth-grade dance class where students are learning how movement can be developed from an emotional intent, the teacher satisfies herself that students understand that movement may define an emotion, then moves to the next part of the lesson and engages students in developing two or three examples of simple movement phrases inspired by an emotional intent.

In both of these examples, the teacher makes a decision to continue with the planned lesson *based on evidence*. In the event that the students had not shown a clear understanding, the teachers' actions would have been different. The teacher is implementing Principles 1 and 2, as discussed in Chapter 2: integrating assessment into the process of teaching and learning, and using evidence to move learning forward.

Make Immediate Instructional Adjustments

When teachers decide that immediate instructional adjustments are necessary to keep learning on track, they can choose from a repertoire of strategies, or what in New Zealand is called Deliberate Acts of Teaching (New Zealand Ministry of Education, 2016). Deliberate Acts of Teaching include modeling, prompting, questioning, telling, explaining, directing, and feedback. Knowing which pedagogical action to take in response to evidence is part of connoisseurship in formative assessment (Cowie, 2016), and constitutes a core skill of formative assessment. One New York teacher summed up the value of taking contingent action through immediate instructional adjustments this way: "It becomes a quick fix—you are meeting the student where he or she is, rather than re-teaching the whole class" (third-grade teacher, personal communication, 2008). Let us examine the Deliberate Acts of Teaching in more detail.

Modeling

Purposeful modeling can be a powerful pedagogical response to evidence of learning. Some examples: In the eighth-grade dance class discussed above, if the teacher had decided that students didn't solidly understand how movement may define an emotion, the teacher might model several movement phrases inspired by emotional intent. In a second-grade class in which students are learning how cloud types can predict weather, the teacher asks the students to write predictions based on their cloud observations. As they do this, he notices that some of their predictions do not make sense and that they lack causal reasoning. The action he takes in response to this information is to model writing predictions using evidence, illustrating his process through a think-aloud. In a case of students having difficulty playing an instrument with the right rhythm, the teacher could model what it needs to sound like by playing a segment of the piece.

Prompting

Prompting involves encouraging students to use their existing knowledge to make their own connections and find their own solutions. For example, in mathematics if students are stuck on a problem, a prompt might be: "Remember when you solved the problem with directed numbers. Think about how you did that and make some connections to this problem." Or the teacher might prompt a discussion among students in response to their difficulty by saying, "I want you to discuss what you need to know in order to solve the problem." In the context of reading, when a student is having difficulty making sense of a text, the teacher might say, "Think about what you already know about this topic and use that to help you figure out what the author is saying."

Questioning

This Deliberate Act of Teaching is one that teachers use most across all content areas. Questioning has two functions: One is for assessment purposes and the other is in response to assessment information. Questions for assessment purposes are intended to gauge the current status of student learning with respect to learning goals and criteria. These questions can be written formal questions or informal verbal questions as part of an assessment conversation. Questions become a Deliberate Act of Teaching when they are used to advance learning in response to the evidence the teachers have obtained; that is, they are intended as a pedagogical response. They become effective pedagogical responses when they are directed toward helping students to meet a learning goal, they are centered on students' thinking, there is adequate wait time for students to think through their ideas, students' ideas are valued and not transformed by evaluative comments that suggest the responses were inadequate, and appropriate follow-up questions are used to extend students' thinking (New Zealand Ministry of Education, 2016).

Questioning that assists students' learning is very different from the all-too-common initiation-response-evaluation (IRE) approach (Cazden, 1988; Mehan, 1979). The IRE method of questioning is focused on correct answers rather than on supporting learning. For example, in an attempt to get his class to recognize the topic of a poem, a teacher asks the students, "What do you think this poem is about?" So far, so good—this question potentially invites students' ideas. However, when a student responds with her idea, the teacher says, "Any other ideas? She's not right," essentially cutting short an exploration of students' thinking.

The example given in Table 5.1 includes both prompts and questions that a high school teacher might use in response to evidence of learning that suggests students have misconceptions and challenges during a lesson focused on students' recognizing and drawing two-dimensional cross-sections at different points along a plane of a representation of a sphere (Q1), a regular tetrahedron (Q2), and a cube (Q3) (MARS, Shell Center, 2015). These prompts and questions enable students to rethink and revise their solutions.

Table 5.1 Issues and Questions for High School Geometry Unit

Common Issues	Suggested Questions and Prompts
No drawings of the shape of the surface of the water	• Now provide some diagrams to show the shape of the surface of the water as the water level changes. • What is the shape of the surface of the water when the vessel is almost full/empty/half full? Draw these shapes.
Confusion between two-dimensional representation of the shape and two-dimensional representation of the surface of the water For example: The student draws two concentric circles, one representing the shape and the other representing the surface area of the water (Q1). Or: The student draws several vertical cross-sections of the sphere, each with different water levels (Q1).	• Your drawings do not need to include the shape of the vessel, just the shape of the surface of the water. • Imagine looking down on the vessel as the water flows out of it. Sketch the shape of the surface of the water.

Table 5.1 Continued

Common Issues	Suggested Questions and Prompts
Description lacks precision For example: The student does not state the radius of the largest circle or when this occurs (Q1). Or: The student does not state that the triangles will be equilateral as the level of the water changes (Q2). Or: The student does not state how the dimensions of the rectangle change as the level of the water changes (Q3).	• What is the radius of the largest circle? When does this occur? • What can you say about the properties of the triangles? • How do the dimensions of the rectangle change? • What are the dimensions of the biggest rectangle? When does this occur?
The drawn shape lacks precision For example: The student draws a series of congruent triangles (Q2). Or: The student draws rectangles that show the width *and* length changing as the level of the water flows out of the vessel (Q3).	• Imagine looking down on the tetrahedron/cube when it is three quarters full, then when it is half full. What has changed about the shape of the surface of the water? • What are the dimensions of the shape when the cube/sphere is half full?
Difficulty representing the middle section of the cube (Q3)	• Imagine the vessel is half full of water. What is the shape of the surface of the water? • What can you say about the dimensions of this shape?
Assumption that because the shape is a cube the shape of the surface of the water will be squares (Q3)	• What determines the width and length of the shape of the surface of the water?

In the next example, pairs of sixth-grade English language learners are reading an article from a health magazine in which the author wishes to persuade readers that, contrary to a lot of advertising, energy drinks are not good for them (Educational Testing Service and National Center for Research on Evaluation, Standards, and Student Testing, 2013). Once the students have read the article and discussed what they think it is about, they answer a series of questions focused on the language and structure of persuasive text. As the teacher engages with pairs to discuss their written responses, she asks questions to address issues she is observing related to students' language and knowledge of text structure (Table 5.2).

In both examples we see the prompts and questions that the teachers used in response to issues that arose during the lesson. In each case, the teacher's response is

Table 5.2 Issues and Questions for Sixth-Grade ELA Unit

Issues Revealed by Evidence	*Questions and Prompts*
Not referencing sentences from the article that take an evaluative stance (*unfortunately . . . advertisements are aimed . . . but the caffeine in energy drinks actually . . .*).	Can you show me some words and sentences in the text that help you know what the author's position is on energy drinks?
Over-reliance on visuals in the text to determine their answer (e.g., deriving their answer only from the bottle image).	Some text near the image helps you understand what happens when you drink too much caffeine. Can you find those sentences? What words in those sentences tell you what happens?
Not using an understanding of the genre text structure to determine the main argument.	What are clues in the text we have discussed in class that could help you determine the main argument?
Having difficulty in perspective shifts in the text.	Who is the author talking about in this sentence? Why is she talking about them? Look at the next sentence. Who is the author talking about here? Why is she talking about them?

contingent upon the learners' current status and designed to support the students to move forward. Knowing the right questions to ask as a teaching tool will be dependent on teachers' content knowledge and on their knowledge of how students learn that content. Thinking in advance of a lesson about what the range of students' likely responses might be can assist teachers in being prepared to ask the right questions in the moment that can support and extend learning.

Telling

Notice that, in the math example above, some of the responses include telling, for instance, "draw these shapes" and "your drawing does not need to include the shape of the vessel." Sometimes, simply telling students something may be the most effective way to keep learning momentum going. The idea of telling is to fill a gap at that moment to enable the student to progress. Other examples of telling are:

- Find another source that supports your conclusion.
- You need to measure to find the length of shadows.
- Read the question again, and pay attention to the words "*with evidence from the text.*"
- If you are having difficulty spelling some of these words, put the online dictionary on your desktop.
- That word means _____. Now continue reading.
- Experiment some more and find a pattern.

The telling response needs to be used judiciously, at moments when the students need some quick information in order to move on, and obviously not at points when students need to deepen or extend their thinking.

Explaining

Explanations go beyond telling. In the reading example with English learners, the teacher could have decided that a better strategy in response to students not using genre text structure would be to explain how they could use the text's introduction and conclusion to determine the main argument. Similarly, in the math example discussed above, instead of asking the students the question about the radius of the largest circle and when it occurs, the teacher could decide that an explanation about the radius of the largest circle is a more appropriate response for particular students. In a history lesson when students are evaluating an 1898 newspaper article about Spain sinking the USS *Maine*, a teacher might decide that the students need an explanation of yellow journalism to help them better evaluate the text. These decisions are judgment calls that teachers make in the moment, based on their knowledge of the students and whether a question or an explanation is the best option to help advance learning.

Crafting an explanation for students in response to evidence is a non-trivial skill. Teachers need to think carefully about how to convey what they want students to understand. For example, Margaret and her colleagues' research on the math quality and linguistic and discourse features of sixth-grade teachers' explanations of key principles in Algebra I revealed considerable variation in teachers' explanations. Some were mathematically incorrect, others used inappropriate examples and analogies, and several introduced inaccurate vocabulary (Bailey & Heritage, 2017).

Directing

Directing is simply giving a specific instruction. For example, "Turn to your partner and share . . ." or "Start your writing on a new page" or "Make notes in the margin." Like all the Deliberate Acts of Teaching, directing is used deliberately and for a particular purpose, and always in the service of advancing learning.

Providing Feedback

One of the most powerful actions that teachers can take in response to evidence is to provide feedback to students. John Hattie's synthesis of over 800 meta-analyses related to achievement focused on effect sizes, which are indicators of practical significance. Hattie considered programs with effect sizes above 0.4 as worthwhile, with those lower than 0.4 needing further consideration. The influence of feedback has a large effect size of 0.73, slightly greater than teacher-student relations (0.72), whereas class size and ability grouping influences have low effect sizes of 0.21 and 0.12 respectively (Hattie, 2009). We discussed feedback in detail in Chapter 1. Here we show some examples of teacher feedback in response to evidence.

- In a fifth-grade classroom, students are learning about writing arguments. During the course of independent writing, one student requests feedback from her teacher about an issue she is thinking about in her writing: Can she put two rhetorical questions consecutively? The teacher spends some time discussing the issue with the student, and finally they agree that the two questions contain ideas that are connected to her counterargument. The teacher suggests that the student consider how she might combine these ideas in one question, and the student agrees to this plan, which resolves the issue she had identified. Later the teacher checks back with the student to assure

herself that the feedback she provided has been used successfully.
- In a physical education class, the teacher gives this feedback to a student after watching a soccer game: "You were clearly aware of where the players were positioned, because you were constantly looking around you and made good use of that knowledge when you disposed of the ball. Sometimes, though, your disposal was not accurate and the other players missed the ball. In class tomorrow, I suggest you work on drills to improve ball disposal."
- In a science class where students were learning to design a fair test, the teacher reviewed a student's design with him and provided this feedback: "Your design shows you are clear about what you want to measure, and you have listed four factors that should remain constant and one that will change. For your test to be fair, there is one other factor that must remain constant. Can you review your plan and think about what else needs to be constant? I'll be back in a few moments to hear your ideas."

In each of these examples, the teacher provided feedback that did not do the students' thinking for them, but rather gave them a suggestion for how they might improve their learning with their own efforts. The nature of the feedback, how much, and when it is given is dependent on individual students, and is a decision you will need to make about each of your students.

As with all the Deliberate Acts of Teaching, the purpose is to provide the necessary assistance to move students' learning along. However, as we discussed in Chapter 4, if students are not given the opportunity to use the feedback, giving it becomes a useless enterprise. Ensuring that students are given time to use the feedback in the lesson (or possibly for homework) is a must.

Make Plans for Subsequent Lessons

Continuing with the planned lesson or engaging in Deliberate Acts of Teaching involves immediate or near-immediate actions during the course of a class period. In so doing, teachers are enacting assessment Principles 1 and 2: assessment is integrated into the process of teaching and learning, and assessment evidence is used to move learning forward. In addition to these actions, another response is for teachers to use the evidence they have obtained during one class period to plan for the next. For example, in the situation where the physical education teacher provided feedback to one student, she might instead see that many students are having problems with ball disposal and plan to focus on skill building with all students during the subsequent class period. Similarly, rather than providing feedback on one student's design for a fair test (making sure that one factor changes at a time while keeping all other conditions the same) in a science investigation, the teacher might decide that there are a group of students who need more teaching about what a fair test entails, and make plans to work with that group the next day. In the instance when the English learner teacher responds with a question to students to help them think about determining an argument, she might decide that too many students are still shaky in their understanding of genre text structure and plan to do a mini-lesson on this for the whole class to begin the next class period.

As we noted earlier in this book, responding to evidence is part of connoisseurship in formative assessment: Teachers have to make more or less on-the-spot decisions about the best response for individuals, groups, or the whole class. Even when they are planning for the subsequent class period, the turnaround time is short. Making decisions about how to respond to evidence is not an exact science. Fortunately, an attentive teacher will quickly realize when one response didn't lead to the desired result and can select another that might be more effective. The essential point in formative assessment is that there *is* a response. If no action is taken in response to evidence, then formative assessment is not happening.

Students Taking Action: Assessment Strategies That Prompt Corrections, Rethinking, and Revisions Connected to Learning Goals and Success Criteria

It is not enough for feedback to reveal to teachers the gaps in students' knowledge or skills: Feedback must also help learners figure out what to do to improve their work and deepen their learning (Wiliam, 2011). In addition, students must have opportunities to relearn and revise based on feedback, either in class or as homework.

Many assessment tools tell students what is wrong with or weak about their learning and their work. The really good ones explicitly scaffold the taking of action, often by including a directing-type Deliberate Act of Teaching. For example, see Maria Comba's fourth-grade melody rubric in Table 5.3 (Valle, Andrade, Palma, & Hefferen, 2016). Ms. Comba is an elementary school music teacher in Brooklyn, New York. She designed a unit on melody to train students to hear melody lines and to develop skills in notating simple melodies. This unit focused on ear training and melodic dictation. Students were asked to listen

Table 5.3 Maria Comba's Fourth-Grade Melody Rubric

	I've GOT it!	AH-HA... I'm almost there!	I'm getting better!	I need some help, please.
Drawing the Contour	I got it! Not only can I draw the contour, but I can also add details so it starts to look like a melody on the staff.	Ah-ha! I CAN draw the contour correctly. *Now I'm working on* notating some details so it can start to look like a melody line on a staff.	I can draw the contour when it moves in one direction only. *Now I'm working on* "listening for movement" in contours that move in different directions.	*Now I'm working on* "listening for movement." I'm always asking myself if the music sounds like it's moving up the stairs or down the stairs.
Notating the Melody on the Staff	I can notate the melody when given the starting pitch. I used "listening for movement," melodic motion (ascending, descending, step, skip), and solfège to help me.	I can use the starting pitch and melodic motion to help me figure out the movements and relationships of pitches in the melody. *Now I'm working on* writing notes closer to their actual pitch. Using melodic motion and solfège will help.	I can notate the direction of the contour by using melodic motion but cannot place them on the staff as of yet. *Now I'm working on* using the starting pitch to help me place notes on the staff.	*Now I am working on* "listening for movement" and matching it up with melodic motion. I will always follow picture cues with my finger to see if they match.
Singing the Melody	I can sing the melody line given the starting pitch. I used melodic motion and solfège to help me.	I can sing the melody line moving in the right direction but the pitches are not accurate. *Now I'm working on* being more accurate with each individual pitch.	I can sing the contour but cannot match individual notes. *Now I'm working on* using solfège to help me sing the correct pitch.	*Now I'm working on* making sure that my voice is going in the right direction. I'm listening, tracing contours, and echoing.

Note: The "now I'm working on" phrases are your goals for next week.

carefully to a melody in order to draw the shape, or contour, of the melody line. The learning goals for the lesson were to:

1. understand the concept of melody,
2. understand and be able to distinguish between the melody line and the accompaniment,
3. understand how melody is developed,
4. use vocabulary appropriately when speaking about melody.

Notice how the repeated phrase "now I'm working on" in the rubric helps students identify specific areas in need of improvement, goals for their work, and strategies for meeting those goals—all within the rubric itself. The explicitly stated goals and next steps on the rubric give students immediate and appropriate tactics for improving the quality of their work. They also help to develop goal setting, an essential first step in self-regulated learning (Principle 3). The "now I'm working on" phrases also communicate the belief that learning is incremental and effortful—a mastery mindset that lends itself to lifelong learning and self-regulation (Dweck, 2007).

Meghan Phadke, a prekindergarten through fifth-grade music teacher in Manhattan, also blurs the distinction between assessment and instruction by including suggestions for improvement in her checklists. With the goals of having students become more self-directed and learn to play the recorder at their own pace, she asked them, "How do we learn a song? What are the things we need to do as musicians? What are the steps?" (Valle et al., 2016). She then co-created criteria with her students by having them think of specific strategies and mental checks for each criterion that would help them focus their thinking and improve particular aspects of their playing. She took these criteria and strategies and created the self- and peer assessment tools in Table 5.4.

The two checklists in Table 5.4 articulate the criteria for the sound of a song on the recorder when it is played well and the techniques students can use to improve their playing. Students used the checklists by listening to their playing and assessing it using the targeted criteria in the Skill column. If students determined that their playing did not meet the expectation set by those criteria, then they referred

Table 5.4 Meghan Phadke's Third-Grade Recorder Self- and Peer Assessment Checklists

RECORDER SELF-ASSESSMENT			
Name:			
Song Title:			
Skill	*Always*	*Still working*	*How do I fix it?*
Plays with a gentle beautiful tone (no squeaks!)			Check your breath and posture.
Plays correct notes			Use your G clef and hand staff to check each note.
Uses correct fingering			Check fingering chart.
Covers holes completely with finger pads			Check your fingertips for circles.
Plays rhythms correctly			Clap the rhythm and see if it matches.
Plays whole song on the first try			SLOW DOWN.

(Continued)

Table 5.4 Continued

RECORDER PEER ASSESSMENT			
Student completing this form:			
Student playing the recorder:			
Song Title:			
Skill	Always	Still working	How can your partner fix it?
Plays with a gentle beautiful tone (no squeaks!)			
Plays correct notes			
Uses correct fingering			
Covers holes completely with finger pads			
Plays rhythms correctly			
Plays whole song on the first try			

to the "How do I fix it?" column for a specific strategy for improvement. The "How do I fix it?" strategies—checking posture, clapping the rhythm, slowing down the tempo, and so forth—provided immediate, actionable next steps. The same procedure was followed when giving feedback to a peer. In this way, feedback according to this checklist was always targeted, specific, and focused on improvement. Following both self- and peer assessment, students used the feedback to make revisions to their performance.

Ms. Phadke observed that her assessment tools were useful in helping students become more in control of their learning, more independent, and better able to work at their own pace. Because the self- and peer assessments described clear performance criteria and recommended specific strategies for fixing problems, students were often able to troubleshoot and resolve problems without seeking help from her.

A final example of the way in which assessment can support students in taking action and in self-regulating their learning comes from Patricia Applegate, a dance teacher at a public middle school in Brooklyn, New York (Andrade, Lui, Palma, & Hefferen, 2015). Ms. Applegate developed and implemented what she called the *African Dance Unit*. The unit involved groups of students in collaboratively creating two 8-count movement patterns that reflected the general characteristics of African dance: polyrhythm, repetition, isolations of body, low center of gravity in the body, grounded movements, movements done in unison with other dancers, movements from daily life, and differentiation between movements of women and men. The unit complemented a Social Studies unit on African culture, so the theme of each dance was the work that is done in a traditional African society, such as farming, fishing, hunting, and work done in the home. The learning goals were for students to be able to collaboratively create choreography with two 8-count movement patterns that:

- clearly expresses the intent of the dance; and
- uses original movement motifs informed by African dance.

The process goals for her students were to:

- show initiative and independence in rehearsals; and
- discuss possible revisions for dance studies in progress using co-created criteria, keeping intent of dance in mind.

During the four-week African Dance Unit, groups of four students choreographed and performed an eight-count pattern. The class discussed the qualities that they would include in their choreography (e.g., polyrhythms, bent knees, isolation of body parts, and percussion). Once students were familiar with the new vocabulary, Ms. Applegate and her students co-created a list of product criteria that they agreed were important to the quality of movements. Students used the checklist in Figure 5.1 to guide their group self-assessment.

The checklist clearly articulates the product criteria for the dance—for example, exaggerated movements and high energy. But it goes further: This checklist helps students

---

All of you have created eight-count patterns depicting everyday movements that you do in your tribe. Everybody can count the beat, and remember the patterns. Now let's see if we can make it even better! Your group will look at the checklist and choose one criterion you want to focus on.
Will your group:

- _____ **exaggerate** the movements? Try to fully extend your arms, and explore taking larger steps to expand your movements.
- _____ show the **rhythm** of the drum beats in your body? Try to accent the rhythm with a strong body action or even add some vocal sound or body percussion.
- _____ demonstrate high **energy**? Try to jump higher or add your whole body into the movements.
- _____ use different **levels** in your dance? Try to change levels in your movement. If you were up high, try to do some moves down low.
- _____ move in a variety of **directions**? Try to use all the space around you. If you went forward and back, why not try going diagonal or sideways, too?

Figure 5.1 Patricia Applegate's Sixth-Grade Movement Quality Checklist

take action by including suggestions for movements to try in order to meet the standards set by the criteria. In this way, a simple checklist reflects both Principles 2 and 3: Assessment evidence is used to move learning forward, and supports student self-regulation. The use of the checklist meant that the processes of goal setting, group self-assessment, and independent revision (Principle 3) could naturally meld with the creative process of choreography and dance making (Principle 1).

Summing Up and Moving Forward

Our experiences as teacher-researchers have convinced us that formative assessment is one of the most powerful and effective tools that teachers have at their disposal. The elements of formative assessment include clear learning goals and criteria, evidence of learning as it unfolds, feedback, responsive action, and revision. Conversations with students, diagnostic tests, peer and self-assessment, new technologies, and more can be used to provide feedback to students that informs next steps in their learning, and feedback to teachers that can inform adjustments to instruction.

At the beginning of this book, we promised that carefully implemented formative assessment will lead to more learning and skill development, and even higher grades and test scores. By now the basis for that claim is probably apparent: When we think about assessment as feedback that leads to responsive action, and not just as measurement, bold claims about learning make sense. When assessment is integrated into classroom activities (Principle 1), used to move learning forward (Principle 2), and involves students in ways that support self-regulated learning (Principle 3), learning is practically inevitable.

Where should you start to implement more effective formative assessment? We recommend taking inspiration from the interviews of teachers who incorporated formative assessment into their teaching, found here: http://artsasessmentforlearning.org/about-assessment/. Click on About Assessment, and then scroll down and click on Chapter 11. Those teachers give sound advice, such as:

- Keep it manageable by beginning with one unit or topic. One teacher, David Paterson, further recommends that you start with just one class, perhaps one "you are very comfortable teaching, and then branch out."
- Angela Fremont echoes our emphasis in Chapter 3 on the importance of articulating your learning goals and success criteria when she says, "Think about what it is you really want to teach. If you have really clear criteria, if your judgments are based on what you want your students to learn, know, and understand . . . , that will help you." Goals and criteria that are grounded in the standards of your discipline will set a strong foundation for everything that follows.
- Several teachers comment on the need to commit to taking the time to teach students to engage in formative assessment, noting that the initial investment of time will pay off in the long run because students become able to "do the work of assessing," as Jonathan Meyers puts it. Explaining, modeling, and providing feedback on students' use of criteria and feedback protocols will pay dividends.

Perhaps Audrey Mullen puts it best: "Try it. Don't be intimidated by it, just say I'm going to give it a try, and more than once or twice. I'm going to try it over and over again until I get it right. It is adjustable . . . you can tweak it until it fits you and your program and your students."

References

Andrade, H., Lui, A., Palma, M., & Hefferen, J. (2015). Formative assessment in dance education. *Journal of Dance Education*, *15*(2), 47–59. doi:10.1080/15290824.2015.1004408

Bailey, A. L., & Heritage, M. (2017). Imperatives for teacher education: Findings from studies of effective teaching for English language learners. In M. Peters, B. Cowie, & I. Menter (Eds.), *A companion to research in teacher education*. Berlin, Germany: Springer.

Cazden, C. B. (1988). *Classroom discourse*. Portsmouth, NH: Heinemann.

Cowie, B. (April 2016). *Connoisseurship in formative assessment*. Presentation at the FAST SCASS Conference, Portland, OR.

Dweck, C. (2007). *Mindset: The new psychology of success*. New York, NY: Ballantine Books.

Educational Testing Service and National Center for Research on Evaluation, Standards, and Student Testing. (2013). *English learner formative assessments, teacher's versions* [Guidance documents]. Retrieved from https://ets.org/research/topics/ella/elfa/teachers_versions/

Hattie, J. (2009). *Visible learning: A synthesis of over 800 meta-analyses relating to achievement*. Oxford, UK: Routledge.

MARS, Shell Center. (2015). *Mathematics assessment project*. Retrieved from http://map.mathshell.org

Mehan, H. (1979). *Learning lessons: Social organization in the classroom*. Cambridge, MA: Harvard University Press.

New Zealand Ministry of Education. (2016). *Deliberate acts of teaching*. Retrieved from http://literacyonline.tki.org.nz/Literacy-Online/Planning-for-my-students-needs/Effective-Literacy-Practice-Years-1-4/Deliberate-Acts-of-teaching

Valle, C., Andrade, H., Palma, M., & Hefferen, J. (2016). Applications of peer and self-assessment in music education. *Music Educators' Journal*, *102*(4), 41–49. doi:10.1177/0027432116644652.

Wiliam, D. (2011). What is assessment for learning? *Studies in Educational Evaluation*, *37*(1), 3–14.

Index

Note: Page numbers in *italics* indicate figures and tables.

actions by students 114, *115*, 116–21, *117–18*, *120*
actions by teachers: continue with lesson as planned 102–3; directing 110–11; explaining 110; make instructional adjustments 103–13; make plans for subsequent lessons 113–14; modeling 103–4; prompting 104; providing feedback 111–13; questioning 105–9, *106–7*, *108*; telling 109
African dance unit 119–21, *120*
Arts Assessment for Learning website 9
ASSISTments 77–8

Blueprints for Teaching and Learning in the Arts 42
building blocks 42

checklists *52*, 52–3, 116–19, *117–18*
classroom assessments, benefits of 1–2; *see also* formative assessments; summative assessments
Classroom Challenges 77
classroom culture 17–21
co-construction of criteria 59–61
college and career readiness standards 2
Common Core State Standards for Mathematics 78
computer-based assessment programs 76–81
connoisseurship 67–9
consequential validity 85
consistency of principle in formative assessment 26

Index 125

construct maps/models, goals derived from 44–7
construct validity 82–3, 84–5
coordinate grids mathematics lesson 68, 68–69
criteria: articulating 39–40; co-construction of 59–61; overview 47–8; performance 48, 50–1; product 48, 49, 51–5, 58; self-regulation and 59

deep learning 2
Deliberate Acts of Teaching 103, 105, 112, 113
DIAGNOSER interactive program 72
diagnostic items: based on model of cognition 46–7; collecting and interpreting evidence of learning from 70–73; on fractions 71; overview 33–4
directing 110–11

ELA class, feedback in 111–12
ELA unit, sixth-grade, issues and questions for 108
elementary mathematics lesson, principles of formative assessment in 30–2
evidence of learning: actions based on 101, 103, 113–14; overview 65–7; quality of 81–4; using 86–7
evidence of learning, collecting and interpreting: from diagnostic items 70–3; from parallel tests 74–6; from peers 91–2, 92, 93, 94–5; from student self-assessments 87–9, 90, 91; as students work 67–70, 68; with technology 76–81
explaining 110

FACT 77
fairness in formative assessment 83, 86

feedback: classroom culture and 17–21; as core element of formative assessment 3, 9–12; examples of effective and ineffective 12; from peers 91–2, 92, 94–5; providing 111–13; revision after 11–12; self-regulated learning and 16, 17; student interpretations of 95–7
formative assessments: implementing 122–3; as integrated processes (Principle 1) 29, 32, 33, 34, 67–70; overview 121; purpose of 3; as supporting moving forward (Principle 2) 29, 30, 32, 33, 34; as supporting self-regulation (Principle 3) 29–30, 32, 33–4; *see also* principles of formative assessment
fractions, diagnostic items on 71

geometry unit, high school, issues and questions for 106–7
goals: articulating 39–40; from learning progressions 43–7; self-regulation and 59; from standards 40–3
goal setting: by students 15; by teachers 40
gradation rubric 6, 7, 8
grading 4–5
guiding questions 5–6, 26–7

high school geometry unit, issues and questions for 106–7

identities as learners 20–1
initiation-response-evaluation approach 105
instructional adjustments, making 103–13
integrated process, formative assessment as (Principle 1) 29, 32, 33, 34, 67–70

Kindergarten Writing Checklist 52

Ladder of Feedback protocol 92, 93, 94–5
learning: deep 2; mastery 74–6; prospective view of 25–6; self-directed 9; *see also* evidence of learning; self-regulated learning
learning intentions/goals/targets *see* goals
learning progressions/trajectories: as frameworks for interpretation of evidence of learning 87; goals derived from 43–7
lesson plans: continuing with 102–3; making 113–14

mastery learning 74–76
mathematics units: coordinate grids 68, 68–9; elementary, principles of formative assessment in 30–2; high school geometry, issues and questions for *106–7*
mentor texts 28, 60
middle school classroom, principles of formative assessment in 27–30
modeling 103–4
models 51
motivation 35–37
moving forward, formative assessment as supporting (Principle 2) 29, 30, 32, 33, 34
multiple-choice items 46, 70–1
music: melody unit, rubric for 114, *115*, 116; recorder self- and peer assessment checklists 116–19, *117–18*

New York City Department of Education, *Blueprints for Teaching and Learning in the Arts* 42

online assessment response tools 79–81

parallel tests, collecting and interpreting evidence of learning from 74–6
peers, collecting and interpreting evidence of learning from 87–8, 91–2, *92*, *93*, 94–5
performance criteria 48, *49*, 50–1
persuasive essays: rubric for 56–7; scaffolded self-assessment of drafts of 90; writing 27–30
physical education class, feedback in 112
practice tests, parallel tests compared to 75
principles of formative assessment: diagnostic items and 33–4; in elementary mathematics lesson 30–32; in middle school classroom 27–30; overview 26
prior knowledge 41
process-oriented feedback 10, 11
product criteria 48, *49*, 51–5, 58
prompting 104
prospective view of learning 25–6
Pythagorean theorem, performance and product criteria for unit on *49*

quality of evidence of learning 81–4
questioning 105–9, *106–7*, *108*

recorder self- and peer assessment checklists 116–19, *117–18*
reliability in formative assessment 83–4, 85–6
researcher-developed assessment technologies 77–8
revision after feedback 11–12
rubrics: features of 6, 7; gradation 6, 7, 8; for music melody unit

Index 127

114, *115*, 116; as product criteria 53–5; for self-assessment 89; for seventh-grade persuasive essay 56–7; solar system scoring 45

science class, feedback in 112
self-assessment 87–9, 90, 91, *117–18*
self-directed learning 9
self-efficacy beliefs 35–7
self-evaluation/grading 88
self-level feedback 10–11
self-regulated learning (SRL): classroom assessment and 11; formative assessment and 12–16; model of *17*; self-assessment in 91; supporting students to develop 34–7
self-regulation: formative assessment as supporting (Principle 3) 29–30, 32, 33–4; goals, criteria, and 59
self-regulation-level feedback 10, 11
seventh-grade persuasive essays, rubric for 56–7
SimScientists 78
sixth-grade ELA unit, issues and questions for *108*
solar system: diagnostic item *46*; scoring rubric *45*
SRL *see* self-regulated learning
standards: learning goals derived from 40–3; limitations of, for formative assessment 43–4
statement cards 69–70

students: goal setting by 15; interpretations of feedback by 95–7; self-assessments, collecting and interpreting evidence of learning from 87–89, 90, 91; supporting to develop self-regulated learning 34–7; work of, collecting and interpreting evidence of learning from 67–70, *68*; *see also* actions by students
summative assessments: learning progressions and 44, 46; parallel tests 74; purpose of 3; reputation of 4–5

task-level feedback 10
teacher connoisseurship 67–9
teachers, goal setting by 40; *see also* actions by teachers
technology, collecting and interpreting evidence of learning with 76–81
telling 109
Two Stars and a Wish approach 92, 93

validity in formative assessment 82–3, 84–5
visual arts unit example 5–9

Why Things Sink and Float unit (Stanford Educational Assessment Laboratory) 67
worked examples 51

Taylor & Francis eBooks

Helping you to choose the right eBooks for your Library

Add Routledge titles to your library's digital collection today. Taylor and Francis ebooks contains over 50,000 titles in the Humanities, Social Sciences, Behavioural Sciences, Built Environment and Law.

Choose from a range of subject packages or create your own!

Benefits for you

» Free MARC records
» COUNTER-compliant usage statistics
» Flexible purchase and pricing options
» All titles DRM-free.

Benefits for your user

» Off-site, anytime access via Athens or referring URL
» Print or copy pages or chapters
» Full content search
» Bookmark, highlight and annotate text
» Access to thousands of pages of quality research at the click of a button.

REQUEST YOUR FREE INSTITUTIONAL TRIAL TODAY

Free Trials Available
We offer free trials to qualifying academic, corporate and government customers.

eCollections – Choose from over 30 subject eCollections, including:

Archaeology	Language Learning
Architecture	Law
Asian Studies	Literature
Business & Management	Media & Communication
Classical Studies	Middle East Studies
Construction	Music
Creative & Media Arts	Philosophy
Criminology & Criminal Justice	Planning
Economics	Politics
Education	Psychology & Mental Health
Energy	Religion
Engineering	Security
English Language & Linguistics	Social Work
Environment & Sustainability	Sociology
Geography	Sport
Health Studies	Theatre & Performance
History	Tourism, Hospitality & Events

For more information, pricing enquiries or to order a free trial, please contact your local sales team:
www.tandfebooks.com/page/sales

 The home of Routledge books

www.tandfebooks.com

For Product Safety Concerns and Information please contact our EU representative GPSR@taylorandfrancis.com
Taylor & Francis Verlag GmbH, Kaufingerstraße 24, 80331 München, Germany

www.ingramcontent.com/pod-product-compliance
Lightning Source LLC
Chambersburg PA
CBHW061844300426
44115CB00013B/2499